Foretelling the Future

Foretelling the Future

T Wynne Griffon

MALLARD PRESS

ISBN 0-7924-5706-4

Printed in Hong Kong

Designed by Tom Debolski
Edited and captioned by Annie McGarry

Below: A metaphysical seeker encounters a new realm of knowledge. This woodcut is popularly thought to date from the fifteenth or sixteenth century, but was probably the handiwork of the nineteenth-century Frenchman, Camille Flammarion, an advocate of astrology.

CONTENTS

Introduction

D ivination, the art of predicting the future, has intrigued mankind since the dawn of time, and records of varied forms of divination can be found in all cultures. The leaders of ancient Greece, for example, consulted oracles before waging war. Elsewhere, people have used objects ranging from tea leaves and crystal balls to live chickens and animal entrails, to unlock the mysteries of the present and the future.

Everyone has had, or knows someone who has had, an unexplainable experience happen to them. There may not be indisputable facts that substantiate such paranormal occurrences; but neither is there any evidence to the contrary. These ancient augury rituals provide a window into a world that is normally obscured from us. The insights garnered through this window may come from our own psyches, or be a communication from another spirit. Or it may be something else entirely, beyond our limited understanding of such matters. Used with proper perspective, these ancient traditions may enhance our understanding of the world around us.

The Universal Appeal of Astrology

Astrology, the study of the stars' influence upon nature and mankind, has been practiced since the earliest civilizations. One of the earliest known examples of a horoscope belonged to Rama, a man born before 3102 BC. Throughout history, astrology has been accorded a place of honor by philosophers and rulers. Indeed, there is no corner of the Earth where people have not read what James Gaffarel, astrologer to Cardinal Richelieu, termed 'the handwriting on the wall of heaven.'

The technical name for astrology is 'The Science of the Decrees of the Stars.' Not until the nineteenth century was any precise distinction made between an astronomer and an astrologer—and each was presumed to possess the knowledge peculiar to the other.

Allusions to astrology are scattered throughout Shakespeare's plays. One character complains: 'It is impossible that anything should be as I would have it; for I was born, Sir, when the Crab was ascending; and all my affairs go backwards.'

Many powerful leaders have consulted the stars.

Caesar was informed by the Sortes Antiatinae that 'he should beware of Cassius.' Caesar, of course, was murdered as a result of Cassius' plot against him. The mathematician Spurina warned Caesar that his Mars threatened violence during the Ides of March, and the outcome is, as they say, history.

A dramatic incident recorded in the history of Rome is the interview between Agrippina, the mother of Nero, and a Chaldean astrologer. This scheming woman asked the stars the outcome of her life's ambition, to make her son the emperor of Rome. The astrologer cast the nativity and rendered the following judgment: 'If he reigns, he shall kill his mother.'

Without a moment's hesitation, Agrippina hissed back: 'Let him kill me so that he but reigns!' Needless to say, the stars gave honest judgment, and Nero grew up to be a practicing astrologer.

Nostradamus was the most famous of the French astrologers, as well as physician to King Henry II and Charles IX. His prophecies, set down in a pamphlet, were read all over the world. Although he died in 1566, he prophesied the rise and fall of the Third Reich (1933-1945), the assassinations of the Kennedy brothers (1963 and 1968), the Gulf War of 1991, the French Revolution and the advent of Napoleon, of whom Nostradamus gave a

Previous page: *According to astrologer James Gaffarel, the stars contain the 'hand-writing on the wall of heaven.' The brighter stars in this view are the seven Pleiades, who serve as the nose ring for the constellation Taurus, the bull.*

Above: *First Lady Nancy Reagan often consulted astrologer Joan Quigley about events concerning her husband, President Ronald Reagan.*

very accurate description. Nostradamus' prediction of the London fire in 1666 is as follows:
> 'The blood o' th' just requires,
> Which out of London reeks,
> That it be raz'd with fires,
> In year threescore and six.'

The Great Plague had swept through London the year before, claiming the lives of nearly 100,000 Londoners.

Adolf Hitler, born under the sign of Aries on 20 April 1889, was a believer in astrology, as were many other persons of high position within the German Reich between 1933 and 1945. In 1940, the British Foreign Secretary, Lord Halifax, hired Hitler's former astrologer, Ludwig von Wohl, as a consultant on Hitler's horoscope. One of the major astrologers in the service of the Reich was Karl Ernst Krafft, one of whose predictions supposedly saved the Fuhrer from an assassination attempt in November 1939. This service did not stop Rudolf Hess from arresting Krafft in June 1941, as part of an official campaign against astrology.

During April 1945, when the Nazi empire was on the verge of collapse, Hitler had two horoscopes done—his own and that of the Reich. The astrologers suggested victory would be snatched from the jaws of defeat. It seems that Hitler's astrologers,

not wanting to be the bearers of bad news, had given him false information in order to save their own lives.

In May 1988, it was revealed that former US President Ronald Reagan and his wife Nancy were using the stars to guide their tenure in the White House. After San Francisco astrologer Joan Quigley predicted the 30 March 1981 assassination attempt during which Mr Reagan was wounded, presidential appearances were no longer scheduled without first consulting Quigley. In 1987, Quigley picked the precise hour for the signing of the historic treaty with the Soviet Union which limited the number of intermediate nuclear weapons in Europe. To this end, she cast the horoscopes of both President Reagan (Aquarius) and Soviet Premier Mikhail Gorbachev (Pisces).

Tortured as a sorcerer in one era, ridiculed as a charlatan in another and raised to high honors in more generous times, the astrologer today continues to read the writing in the sky.

Above, left: Michel de Nostredame, better known as Nostradamus, is history's most famous seer.

Left: Adolf Hitler, a Taurus on the Aries cusp with Leo in the tenth house and a Libra ascendant, was born on 20 April 1889.

Above: The signs of the zodiac adorn this building on the Piazza San Marco in Venice, Italy.

THE HOROSCOPE

A horoscope is a map or diagram of the heavens cast for a particular moment of time and read according to well-established rules. The horoscope is calculated by a mathematical process. Predictions are deduced from the horoscope 'according to a certain chain of causes which for ages past have been found uniformly to produce a correspondent train of effects,' to quote Raphael's A Manual of Astrology.

The annual revolution of the Earth around the sun is divided into the 360 degrees of a circle. The 12 equal subdivisions of the circle are known as the signs of the zodiac. Persons born on the 'cusp,' or line, between two signs of the zodiac have qualities found in both those signs. The cusp refers to the last few days of a departing sign, but mainly to the first week of the incoming sign. While the new sign is gaining its ascendancy, the influence of the old persists, but gradually loses its hold day by day, until the seventh day, when the new sign is in full control.

For fuller interpretation of the signs of the zodiac, they have been divided into periods of approximately 10 days, called the 'decans' or 'decantes,' which cover modifications of individual traits. These are attributed to minor planetary influences, which temper the ruling influence of the period. A study of these is therefore helpful in forming an accurate horoscope, but they are always regarded as subordinate to the ruling planet.

From the earliest days of astrology, there has been much interest in the 'wanderers,' which follow their own paths among the fixed constellations forming the signs of the zodiac. These were simply the celestial bodies that were continually visible from Earth: the sun, the moon, Mercury, Venus, Mars, Jupiter and Saturn.

Each sign of the zodiac is ruled by one planet. The sun governs Leo, while the moon holds sway over Cancer. The other planets each govern two signs: Mercury controls Gemini and Virgo, Venus influences Taurus and Libra, Mars dominates Aries and Scorpio, Jupiter rules Sagittarius and Pisces, and Saturn governs Capricorn and Aquarius. In recent centuries, however, some astrologers have seen fit to reassign Aquarius to Uranus and Pisces to Neptune. No astrological affiliation is usually attributed to Pluto.

Although the signs of the zodiac make up only a fraction of astrological lore, the characteristics of individuals born under each sign are common knowledge in modern popular culture.

Below: The Crab Nebula in Taurus. The constellation of Taurus is said to represent Jupiter when he assumed the form of a bull and bore the mortal Europa away to Crete on his back.

Aries *The Ram*

The first sign of the zodiac is represented by the head and horns of the ram. It is a symbol of offensive power—a weapon of the gods, an implement of the will. The Babylonians sacrificed rams during the period when the sun occupied this sign, which occurs annually from 21 March to 20 April.

Aries, a fire sign, is ruled by Mars and exalted by the sun. Though quick to anger, Rams calm easily. They are quick witted, and enjoy music and entertainment. They say the right thing at the right time. They are keen students who have the ability of applying what they learn to their best advantage.

In business, Rams are especially suited to being salespeople, and their drive is valuable in real estate and financial fields. Rams are fine actors, capable lawyers and statesmen, and are gifted with artistic and literary talents.

In love and marriage, Aries persons find harmony and understanding with those born in Leo, Sagittarius or under their own sign. Marriages with Gemini or Libra are well suited to the Aries temperament.

Taurus *The Bull*

The second sign of the zodiac is represented by the head and horns of a bull. The sun is in Taurus annually from 21 April to 20 May. Ironically, considering the extremely masculine image of the bull, this earth sign is ruled by Venus and exalted by the

Gemini mind does revel in contradictions. Gemini people run hot and cold. Friendliness may turn to mistrust when they encounter problems. They are unconventional and skeptical. The Twins may suffer from misplaced enthusiasm, causing them to neglect real opportunities while they pursue something else. Above all, Geminis should conserve and utilize their gains. For though they picture each success as building to even greater heights, they may overlook the obstacles that can ruin such hopes.

In business, Gemini people fit almost anywhere. They are good salespeople, promoters and successful speculators. They do well in advertising, publishing, television, transportation and other fields where they must keep up with trends.

In love and marriage, Gemini and Libra are well suited, as are Gemini and Aquarius. Some restraining force is needed, however, due to the wavering natures in all the signs involved. Gemini gains drive from an Aries marriage and exuberance from a mate born under Leo. Gemini and Sagittarius form an unusually good marital combination.

Cancer *The Crab*

The fourth sign of the zodiac is symbolized by the folded claws of a crab, thought by Nicholas DeVore to symbolize the joining together of male and female essence.

The sun is in Cancer annually from 21 June to 22 July. A water sign, Cancer is ruled by the moon and, in fact, Cancerians are occasionally referred to in literature as 'moon children.'

Cancerians cling to tradition, yet their moods— and even their purposes—may become as changeable as the moon itself. These people are home centered, and are fond of family life and domestic tranquility, but they also enjoy travel and adventure. Cancerians' great determination and perse-

moon. Strength is the predominating feature of this sign. An excess of strength, however, produces a stubborn, firm-set nature. The governing planet, Venus, emotional and fraught with primitive urges, furthers these Taurean trends rather than tempering them.

In business, the practical mind of Taurus can succeed in all mechanical lines, as engineers, builders and contractors. Often mathematically minded, they are capable cashiers and accountants. Their trustworthy natures, once recognized, may raise them to high positions in financial circles. They are good teachers, due to their natural empathy. Their artistic ability is on the practical side, producing photographers and landscape architects.

In love and marriage, Taurus and Scorpio prove ideal partners, because their strengths and weaknesses complement one another's. Virgo's analytical ability allows for an understanding of Taurus' complex nature. Libra adds good judgment to a union, but there is an element of uncertainty. Taurus and Capricorn are a very fine marital combination.

Gemini *The Twins*

The third sign of the zodiac is represented by two pieces of wood bound together, symbolic of the unrelenting conflict of contradictory mental processes. The sun is in Gemini annually from 21 May to 20 June. Ruled by Mercury, Gemini is an air sign.

A dual nature is the *sine non qua* of the Twins sign. While cases of split personality are very rare, the

Above: *A beautiful full moon. The moon, which rules Cancer, symbolizes irregular forms, pale silvery hues and the Archangel Gabriel. Those born under Cancer are often referred to as Moon children.*

Right: *Marlon Brando, born 3 April 1924, manifests his Aries tendencies by being an entertainer and by being very self-contained, living semi-reclusively on an island.*

Left: Rock star Sting, born 2 October 1951, is a perfect illustration of Librans' proclivities as singers, musicians and actors.

Below: Leo is ruled by the sun, and those born under this sign share in the sun's brilliance and warmth.

of this type fall victim to their own shortcomings, the result can prove disastrous.

Leos love the spotlight, perhaps because to them it is the sun in miniature. They insist upon charting their own course and do so with an inherent vigor. They override their own faults so naturally that they sometimes are not even aware of them.

Leo people enjoy outdoor life and crave the warmth of the sun. Indolence is the greatest of drawbacks to the Leo temperament. Leos will revel in ease and luxury until they are forced to action, either through necessity or their own self-imposed demands.

In business, Leo offers unlimited prospects. Along strictly commercial lines, Leos excel in anything requiring promotion or enthusiastic development. Leos' contagious spirits make them capable hotel managers, restauranteurs, real estate developers, publishers and executives.

Leos succeed because they have a flair for showmanship which can sway audiences as well as clients. Many noted actors were born under this sign, and, in the literary field, they have a tendency toward the dramatic.

In love and marriage, the Leo exuberance is not always harmonious. Leos are perhaps best suited to Aries, Sagittarius or Aquarius, but they also have excellent marital prospects with Cancer and Virgo, as well as those of their own sign.

verance causes them to go to extremes. Despite some seemingly contradictory characteristics, Cancer can be developed into one of the best of the signs by persons who subordinate the morbid side and refuse to dwell in the past.

In business, people of this sign succeed along established lines. They do well as manufacturers and merchants, because quality is important to them, and they take pride in what they produce. However, they must learn to be aggressive. Otherwise they can vacillate and find themselves left far behind.

Professionally, they are good teachers, librarians, historians and scientists. They are capable lawyers and politicians. Many Cancerians rise to a high rank in art, literature and music.

In love and marriage, the home-loving nature of Cancer is an important factor, but it must be remembered that Cancer mates can suffer through neglect. Cancer and Capricorn are usually admirably suited to matrimony. Cancer and Pisces are a good combination; while Scorpio and Libra also do well with Cancer.

Leo *The Lion*

The symbol for the fifth sign of the zodiac is an emblem of the sun's fire, heat or creative energy. It is possibly derived from an emblem representing the phallus, used in ancient Dionysian mysteries. The sun is in Leo annually from 23 July to 22 August. A fire element, Leo is ruled, of course, by the sun itself.

Both ambition and idealism are present under Leo, for the brilliance of this sign reflects its governing planet, the sun. But Leo, as well as being high-minded, can be high-handed. When people

Virgo *The Virgin*

The sixth sign of the zodiac, Virgo is usually depicted as a young girl holding a green branch, an ear of corn or a spike of grain. The sun is in Virgo annually from 23 August to 22 September. Ruled by swift, sure Mercury, Virgo is an earth sign.

Virgo people have inquiring minds that will not rest until they have learned all they want to know about a subject. They are skilled at drawing information from people, and then filling in from other sources or extrapolating facts into a remarkably accurate picture.

Order and harmony are essential to the Virgo mind. Therefore, Virgo people should simplify their lives and purposes, or they will bog down under a mass of detail that their exacting minds cannot ignore. The less little things bother them, the greater their capacity for higher aims. Virgo people are usually tolerant, but once blind to their own faults, they may become even more opinionated than those whom they criticize.

Imagination rules the Virgo mind, making them fearful of accidents, illness and financial problems. They are sensitive to pain and any kind of suffering, which makes them superficially sympathetic to those who experience misfortune.

In business, Virgo people are suited to special lines, where their quick minds see new opportunities or productive deals. They are good at evaluating business conditions and market trends. They become good writers, editors, lawyers and professors because they size up things quickly and apply their conclusions ingeniously. Many become architects or designers. As actors, lecturers and salesmen, however, they must overcome their self-consciousness to succeed.

Love and marriage present problems for Virgos because of the exacting, fault-finding and sometimes demanding nature evidenced by this sign. One of the best marital combinations for Virgo is with another of the same sign, as each may understand the other's critical moods. Virgos may find happiness with those born under the sign of Pisces, while Aries, Taurus and Capricorn would also prove compatible. Virgo and Libra could be helpful to each other, but their strong minds might clash.

Above, left: A spiral galaxy in Virgo. The constellation of Virgo is said to represent the story of Erigone, daughter of Icarius, who hanged herself out of grief at the death of her father.

Above: The symbol for Virgo is the Virgin, here represented by Raffaello's Madonna del Cardellino.

Libra *The Scales*

The symbol of Libra, seventh sign of the zodiac, is the scales, emblem of equilibrium and justice. The sun is in Libra annually from 23 September to 23 October. An air sign, Libra is ruled by Venus and exalted by Saturn.

Everything in Libra has to do with balance; therefore, they balance their vulnerability with determination, judgments with empathy. Libra, the sign of justice, is always trying to promote good will and friendship, even if they must go to the extremes they dread. This is actuated by their inherent love of harmony and beauty, a legacy from Venus.

Intuition is a guiding force with Libras and enables them to ferret out deceit and insincerity, no matter how well concealed. However, if they prejudge a matter, or listen to persons in whom they trust or sympathize, Libras can be carried far astray. They are so susceptible to the influence of those who impress them that they will imitate the manners of such persons and assume their traits.

Compassion and understanding are paramount with Libras. They are never deaf to an appeal from family or friends. They will champion the underdog or lost cause, against their sounder judgment.

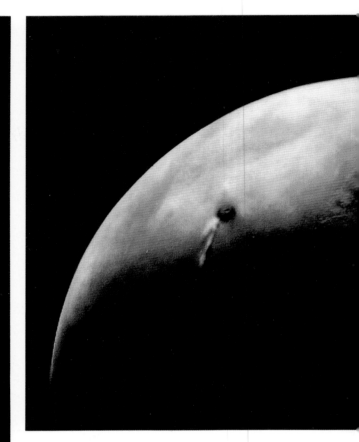

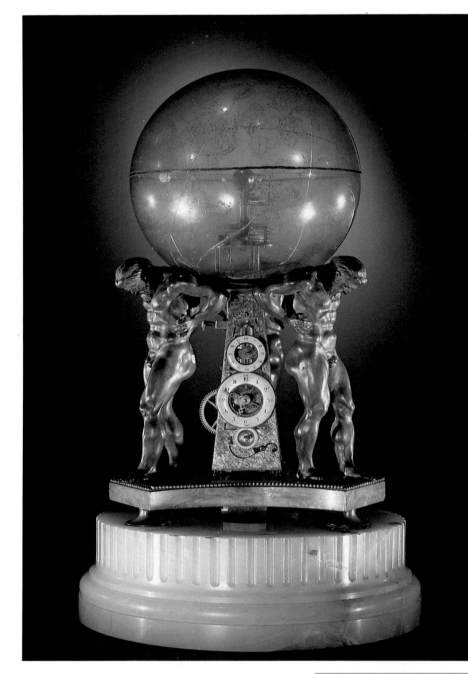

Their greatest need is to equalize matters and produce harmony.

Libras can rise to high positions in business, because their judgment, when properly exercised, is of executive caliber. Similarly, their understanding toward subordinates is a powerful asset. Their intuitive ability makes them excellent merchants, and aids them in speculative fields. However, they should curb their gambling instinct or it may ruin them.

Libras often become inventors, researchers or historians. Their talent to play a part makes them fine actors, and excellent musicians and singers as well. They are talented at many arts and crafts, as well as mathematics. Since Libras like to rely on their own judgment, they should be wary of business partnerships. In love and marriage, Libra does well with Aries because of the latter's drive. Libra gains animation from marriage with Leo. Libra harmonizes with Aquarius, and can benefit from a pairing with Gemini or Scorpio. There is a

Above: *A clock-driven planetary model, or orrery, made in France around* 1800.

natural attraction between Libra and Virgo, but conflicts of interest may result, and Libra and Pisces are seldom a suitable combination. Perhaps the sensitive Libra and jovial Sagittarius are the best pairing of all.

Scorpio *The Scorpion*

The symbol for the eighth sign of the zodiac resembles that of Cancer, but with an arrow on the tail—the sting. It is symbolized by the asp or serpent, harking back to the serpent of the Garden of Eden. For Scorpio, the will governs, or is governed by, the reproductive urge. It is sometimes symbolized by the dragon, and is frequently linked with the constellation Aquilla, the Eagle.

The sun is in Scorpio annually from the second 30-degree arc after the sun's passing of the Fall Equinox from 24 October to 22 November. Scorpio, a water sign, is ruled by Mars and exalted by Uranus.

Theodore Roosevelt, a noted Scorpio, was fond of the slogan, 'Speak softly and carry a big stick,' which aptly summarizes the characteristics of this sign. Scorpio people are quiet, even secretive, in manner, yet very observant. Once roused to action, they are determined, aggressive and dominant, always ready to champion a cause. When they work for the good of others, they rise to great heights and are much respected. But Scorpio people, always well-satisfied with themselves, can easily become domineering and condescending.

Scorpios are blunt, argumentative and natural fighters, and their coolness under fire deceives the opposition and adds to their strength. In the showdown, Scorpio always has to have the upper hand. They need to control their tempers and actions.

Left: *Scorpio is ruled by Mars, the Roman god of war, which accounts for some of Scorpio's more combative qualities.*

Below: *The zodiacal man, from the 'Très Riches Heures du Duc de Berry.'*

Sagittarians are naturally intuitive, with keen foresight, so when they feel sure that something 'can't go wrong' they yield to impulse. However, in their excitement and enthusiasm, they may overlook new problems that might arise. This impetuosity causes Sagittarians great trouble through middle age, when they may become irritable and develop unruly tempers, which can be soothed or restrained only by persons whom they trust. Sometimes they wear themselves down until their recklessness is merely spasmodic. With their stamina depleted, they then fuss from one minor project to another, getting nowhere.

At their best and strongest, Sagittarians insist on seeing things through. Their impulsive actions are contagious, bringing them great popularity and a host of followers. Those who achieve success under this sign are usually neat, methodical and orderly. In business, Sagittarians succeed in anything that provides a multitude of outlets for their active, versatile minds. They like to travel, and do well as prospectors, mining engineers, pilots and sea captains. Imports and exports are good avenues for their progressive, systematic minds. They also do well as bankers and financiers, but in all endeavors they should avoid too many side interests and remember that time is money.

A powerful Scorpio personality can succeed in practically any line. They range from managers of branch offices to the heads of large companies. As heads of investigative bureaus and committees, no other sign can equal them.

In love and marriage, Scorpio finds three strong choices: Taurus, Cancer and Pisces. Scorpio's crusading spirit is admirably seconded by Taurus. The Scorpio boldness fortifies the wavering Cancer disposition and brings Pisces' strong point to the fore. Scorpio may also find harmony with Virgo, while Scorpio's power and Leo's exuberance are a satisfactory combination.

Sagittarius *The Archer*

The sun is in Sagittarius annually from 23 November to 21 December. Ruled by Jupiter, king of all planets, Sagittarius is a fire element.

The ninth sign of the zodiac, Sagittarius was known as Dhanus in Hindu astrology. His symbol, an arrow and a section of bow aiming at the stars, represents aspiration. He is usually pictured as the Centaur, half horse and half man, depicting the conflict between the philosophical mind and the carnal instinct. Sagittarius is said to have been named for the Babylonian god of war.

Being workers, not seekers, Sagittarians accomplish twice as much as others, and will apply themselves to charitable causes with the same energy that they devote to their own aims. When their time is thus divided, they are happiest, because they like doubling their effort. When confronted by adversity or failure, these people can usually stage a remarkable 'comeback' by merely stepping up their activity or their output.

Inventors, writers and large farm operators are all found under Sagittarius. They are quite proficient in scientific and mechanical fields, and partnership with Aries or Gemini can yield great results. The spontaneity of Sagittarius and the exuberance of Leo is also an effective combination, though it may prove less sustained.

In love and marriage, Sagittarius is aptly called 'the bachelor sign' because these freedom-seeking folks can get along quite well on their own. However, they are cheerful, considerate and willing to share burdens, so potentially they might prove to be fine spouses. Sagittarians do well to marry someone born under their own sign or a person born in Gemini, due to the mutual urge toward varied interests. Sagittarius also may marry well with Aries or Leo, who are themselves impetuous to a degree. Sagittarius and Libra are a good marital team, due to their mutual recognition of intuitive qualities.

Capricorn *The Goat*

The tenth sign of the zodiac, Capricorn was considered by the ancients to be the most important of all the signs, and is known in Hindu astrology as Makarar. Its symbol represents the figure by which the sign is usually pictured—that of the forepart of a goat, with the tail of a fish—vaguely suggesting the mermaid. Sometimes Capricorn is depicted as a dolphin, or 'sea goat.'

The sun is in Capricorn annually from 22 December to 20 January. This earth element is ruled by Saturn. Capricorns need encouragement early in life so they may gain confidence and strengthen their genial and witty qualities. The more gregarious they become, the more diversified and realistic their interests, the better they can elude the ever-haunting specters of pessimism and despair.

Self-interest is strong in Capricorn, for these people are used to finding their own way. However, those who are fully matured are by no means selfish. Fear of the future makes them economical, but they share their possessions with others, sometimes too generously. Once a dark mood has passed, a Capricorn manages to forget it. Their desire for success is usually so strong that it rouses petty jealousy on the part of others. If Capricorns do not fall victim to despair, they can outlast their problems and overcome all limitations, and thus become true optimists.

In business, people of this sign are good managers, superintendents, bookkeepers and accountants. Their pragmatic planning makes them good financiers. They succeed in many professions, such as lecturers, teachers and lawyers. They usually evidence strong literary talent. In love and marriage, Capricorn probably does best with Virgo, though Capricorn and Taurus may prove an equally fine union. Capricorn and Aries also promise good love prospects. All three of those signs have qualities which are helpful to Capricorn's fluctuating moods.

¶ Nun saget das buch von den übzigen közen der hímel vnd jrem lauff vnd na turen Vnd hebt an dem hímel an•der do heyſſet das firmament•

Aquarius *The Water Bearer*

The symbol for the eleventh sign of the zodiac is a stream of water, symbolizing the servant of humanity who pours out the water of knowledge to quench the thirst of the world. Aquarians are truth-seekers who wish to communicate what they've learned. Aquarius is thought to represent Ganymede, the young son of Callirhoe, the most beautiful of mortals. Ganymede was carried to heaven by an eagle to act as cup bearer to Jupiter.

The sun is in Aquarius annually from 21 January to 20 February. Before the discovery of the planet Uranus in 1781, Aquarius, an air sign, was identified with the planet Saturn. Since the existence of Uranus has become known, astrologers have been inclined to identify it as the ruler of Aquarius. Still others point to Neptune—discovered in 1846—because the persona of its namesake (Neptune, king of the sea) is so strikingly similar to that of Aquarius.

More famous persons have been born under Aquarius than any other sign. In the great majority of cases they have risen from obscurity or have made up for early failure despite seemingly insurmountable odds. Invariably, they have done this on their own, through the full application of all

Far left: *An illustration from the Augsberg Kalendar of 1484.*

Left: *Capricorn is ruled by the planet Saturn.*

Below: *Distinguished actress Elizabeth Taylor, a Pisces born 27 February 1932, has won two Academy Awards and had two tumultuous marriages to Richard Burton, a Scorpio.*

that they have learned. Self-reliance, confidence and the belief that they are right are the qualities that lay the foundation of the Aquarians' success.

Aquarians who develop the honesty and kind sentiments of their sign are sure to attain great heights. They have mild dispositions and can curb their tempers. They are both active and volatile, and once their ambitions are sparked, they can scale unprecedented heights. The Aquarian's greatest fault is indolence, for if they delay or treat life lazily, they will never get anywhere. They must also maintain their natural, quiet dignity, for without it, they may become boastful and surly.

In business, Aquarians are good bargainers, keen buyers, capable auctioneers and excellent promoters, because they know how to stimulate interest. They do especially well in law and politics. Their mechanical skills are well developed; many noted scientists, as well as famous inventors, have been born under this sign.

In love and marriage, Aquarius does well with most signs, because the Aquarian has an understanding nature. Gemini, Leo and Libra are especially good, as they respond strongly to the sympathies of Aquarius.

Pisces *The Fishes*

The symbol of the twelfth and final sign of the traditional zodiac represents a pair of great seahorses or sea lions, yoked together, who dwell in the innermost regions of the sea. It is also symbolic of life after death, and of bondage—the inhibiting of self-expression, except through others— as well as of the struggle of the soul within the body.

The sun is in Pisces annually from 21 February to 20 March. Traditionally thought to have been ruled by Jupiter, Pisces, a water sign, is more properly affiliated with Neptune, a planet that was unknown to all but a few people until 1846.

Because of their unselfish dispositions, Pisceans sometimes fail to fully realize their own possibilities. The greater their honesty, the more doubtful they become as to their own ability. In turn they become more fearful of the future, which then increases their immediate worries. Subsequently, Pisces people are perhaps the most cautious of all the signs where their own affairs are

concerned. In contrast, however, Pisceans often rely upon the promises of other people and thus are easily and frequently duped. Though they themselves are sincere and trustworthy, they are often blamed for the mistakes of others, who have shunted the burden onto the kindly Pisces person. Often, a Pisces individual becomes the victim of a subtle, cunning plot, which they never suspect.

It is quite easy for another person to hold sway over Pisces, but Pisces is saved by a Jupiter-inspired optimism. Thanks to their jovial dispositions, Pisceans can make their way through deep troubles almost as if they were trifles. Their true worth is always sincerely appreciated by real friends and good people, who help them to accentuate their strong points and even serve as buffers against unscrupulous persons.

In business, Pisceans tend to gravitate to large organizations, where their honesty and executive capacity can be appreciated. They do well in government jobs and scientific pursuits. Many of them also succeed as engineers. They are interested in historical subjects and all forms of nature.

While a marriage between two persons born under Pisces is harmonious, it is difficult for one to bring out the other's more forceful qualities. Pisces would do better in a pairing with Cancer, Virgo or Scorpio, but other signs often prove helpful, with the exception of Libra, which is too prone to weigh the Piscean shortcomings.

The Secrets of the Runes

Long ago, rune-masters and mistresses would travel from town to town, divining the fates and fortunes of the inhabitants with the help of their runic pieces. They dressed in animal skins and the blue cloaks sacred to the god Odin. Odin, lord of death and rebirth, hung from 'Yggdrasil,' the world tree, for nine days, and sacrificed his eye to Mimir, guardian of the well of wisdom, in order to get the Runes. Modern diviners still invoke the name of Odin for divine intervention in their casting and reading.

The Runes, an ancient Germanic alphabet, have always carried magical and divinatory meanings. The word 'Rune' derives from the Old Norse 'run,' which means 'secret.' The Vikings engraved Runes on the hilts of their swords and built them into the walls of their homes to ward off evil. In Scandanavia, shamans used Runes to heal the sick, protect burial mounds and cast spells. Runes also supposedly enabled shamans to fly through the air and communicate with the dead.

Runes are traditionally made out of wood; the sacred ash, yew and oak are the ideal materials.

Flat pebbles and ceramic shards or squares are used as well. Each of the 25 squares are about two inches (five cm) high and ¾ inch (two cm) thick with rounded edges. The symbols are either carved or painted on, usually in red (signifying blood) or blue (because it is the color sacred to Odin) paint. The ancient Rune masters used their own blood.

For the purpose of divination, Runes are mixed in a pouch (typically suede or leather), and then cast onto a flat surface. Those which land face down are ignored. Runes landing in proximity to each other are read as influencing one another. Should a Rune fall with its symbol upside-down from the reader, it is 'reversed.'

THE SACRED MEANINGS OF THE RUNES

Freyja The god of fertility and peace denotes good fortune and harmony. Reversed, Freyja signifies loss, stagnation or discord.

Power Wisdom, knowledge and creative power are signified by this Rune, as well as opportunity, sexuality and good fortune. Reversed, it stands for missed opportunities, physical problems or arrested development.

Thorn (Thor) Thor, the Norse god of strength, symbolizes protection, help and good news. Reversed, Thor implies vulnerability and bad tidings. Because the sign is only a thorn, these problems will be small, but should be tended to; even the King of the Beasts may be crippled if a thorn is not removed.

Odin The appearance of Thor's father in a cast signifies wisdom and the assistance of an older person. It can mean magic, psychic power or initiation. Reversed, this Rune is apt to invoke Odin's sense of mischief. A prankster, particularly an older person, may cause trouble.

Wheel A journey, physical or spiritual, brings progress. Reversed, the Wheel portends delays, lessons or difficult journeys.

Fire The creative fire can signify either the artistic impulse or the passion of love. Reversed, something or someone is extinguishing this fire.

Gift Generosity, brotherhood and intimacy will follow. Reversed, the Rune signifies selfishness and isolation. Friendships are in danger.

Joy A sign of happiness, harmony and positive change. Reversed, there is strife between people. This Rune advises that care be given to prevent troublesome situations.

Hail Unexpected setbacks and illnesses are foretold. Reversed, there will be delays caused by external forces.

Necessity This important Rune advocates patience. Greed or selfish desire will cause problems. Reversed, decisions and commitments must be carefully thought out.

Freyja Power Thorn

Odin Wheel Fire

Gift Joy Hail

Necessity Ice Year

Yew Hearth Protection

Ice Obstacles between people may be physical or emotional, such as a coldness signified by ice. Reversed, steps may be taken to 'melt the ice' and dissolve problems between friends.

Year The cycles of nature and life are represented on this Rune. Effort leads to fruition. Reversed, there are impediments in the natural order which must be removed for matters to reach their optimum conclusion.

Yew The yew tree was sacred to Odin, the lord of death, who gathered souls for the journey to Valhalla. Death is a reminder to cherish life on Earth. Also, death may simply mean a passing of old ways and habits. Reversed, this Rune implies an inability to break destructive habits, or an unhealthy fear of death.

Hearth Traditionally a symbol of home, this Rune signifies mystery and a need to probe situations more carefully. Reversed, secrets are revealed and feelings are openly expressed.

Protection This Rune signifies protection from danger and temptation. Reversed, it indicates some danger which must be avoided, possibly coming from a friend or acquaintance.

The Sun Good health and happiness is predicted, as well as creative powers and guidance. Reversed, the Rune signifies an illness resulting from carelessness.

Tyr Tyr, the god of war, symbolizes courage, energy and a passion which brings happiness. Reversed, it is a sign of frustrating and draining conflicts.

Birth This Rune can refer to significant begin-

Page 21: Though runes are traditionally made of wood, they may also be made of flat pebbles or ceramic tiles, as are these.

nings and growth, as well as a new marriage or an actual birth. Reversed, there is stagnation or obstacles preventing progress.

Horse This Rune signifies travel and change, perhaps a new home or job. A spiritual journey may be in the offing.

Man The image of a human being suggests intelligence, memory and culture, the higher attributes of the race. This Rune also refers to family matters. Reversed, it indicates that the person seeks isolation, especially from family. This Rune can also denote a misuse or disuse of intelligence.

Water This Rune, representing intuition, mystery and the subconscious, indicates psychic awareness and unsuspected creativity. Reversed, sea storms leave one confused and emotional.

Fertility Completion of projects, concepts or achievements on any level. Reversed, development is blocked, and extra effort is required.

Day This is a Rune of awakening and clarity. Success and prosperity will flow in abundance. Reversed, a need for conservative spending habits is augured.

Ancestral Property This Rune refers to inheritances and to property in general. Inherited qualities, abilities and family traditions are referred to as well as material goods. Reversed, it signifies that there are problems with inheritance, difficulties with parents, or a break with family.

Wyrd (Fate) Rune masters' and mistresses' bags contain a blank Rune, signifying mystery and fate. It signifies that there will be information withheld from the querant. Fate may decide the issue.

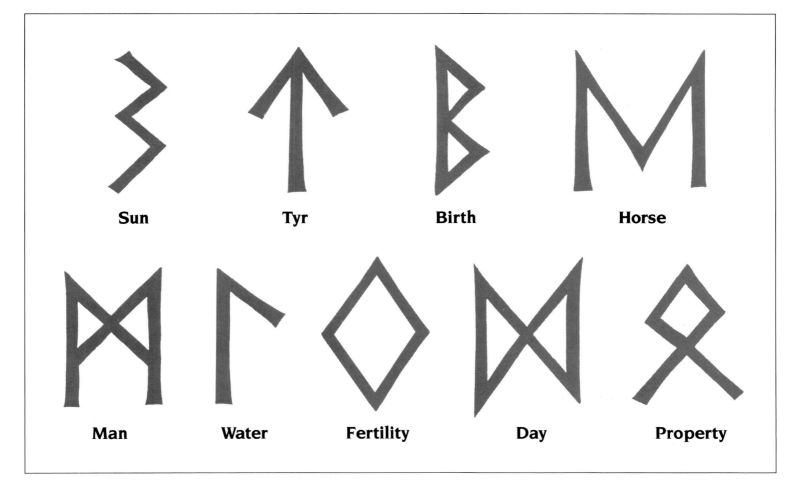

Sun   Tyr   Birth   Horse

Man   Water   Fertility   Day   Property

The Intimate Nuances of Palmistry

Palmistry, the study of the human hand as a method for understanding an individual, is an ancient art. Though there is no conclusive evidence, it seems very likely that the origins of palmistry date back to the ancient Egyptians. The first documented records of palmistry are found in the Indian literature of the Vedic period (circa 2000 BC). In Western cultures, the works of Aristotle (384 to 322 BC) contain the earliest references to palmistry, but both of these cultures suggest an earlier, oral tradition of palmistry. Indeed, palm prints are found in Stone Age cave paintings, suggesting that since the dawn of time, people have been fascinated by the messages contained in their own hands.

The name palmistry is somewhat misleading, for the entire hand—not just the palm—is used to interpret the individual. In fact, palmistry relies on both hands. The left hand is said to indicate the characteristics that one is born with, while the right hand indicates one's nature at the present time. If an individual is left-handed, then the situation is reversed. The shape and feel of the entire

hand, the individual fingers, and the lines and mounts of the palm are all taken into consideration. Once the pieces are put together, palmistry deals with tendencies and probabilities rather than certainties. A palmist will never predict that someone will achieve sudden wealth; instead the emphasis is on the pattern that one's life may follow.

THE SHAPE OF THE HAND

Palm readers have traditionally divided hand shapes into seven categories:

The **elementary** hand is thick and broad, with short fingers. The hand is stiff and awkward and

Previous page: A *soothsayer can read the future in a person's palm.*

Below: Types of hands: (1) elemental, (2) square, (3) spatulate, (4) philosophical, (5) artistic, (6) idealistic, (7) mixed, (8) practical, (9) intuitive, (10) sensitive and (11) intellectual.

indicates a person of low intelligence who relies on brute force. This type of hand is rare.

The **square** hand indicates a practical nature. The hand is actually more rectangular in shape, with squared-off fingertips. The person with this type of hand is orderly and conventional.

The **spatulate** hand is spade-shaped and straight-fingered. This is the hand of the active, energetic individual. The person with the spatulate hand can be found in all fields, but whatever the occupation there is always the urge to be active, to excel and to be original.

The **philosophical** hand has a broad palm and heavy joints on the fingers and thumbs. The fingers are either square or conical. This long and lean hand denotes the thinker, a person with a logical, cautious nature. People with the philosophical hand tend to be introverted and analytical. Often teachers, they are the people who seek knowledge.

The **conical** hand is long and flexible, with tapering fingers. This hand is indicative of an artistic nature. People with a conical hand are creative, sensitive and impulsive rather than methodical. They enjoy companionship and are aware of social issues.

The **pointed** hand (or psychic hand) is even longer and more slender than the conical hand. The pointed hand reveals an idealistic nature and an intuitive mind. People with this sort of hand tend to be dreamers, often with an unrealistic view of the world. They can become martyrs to their own ideas or hold extremist philosophical or religious beliefs.

The **mixed** hand is very common because few people fit neatly into one category. The fingers on a spatulate hand, for example, may belong to two or three different categories. Thus, the palmist must analyze all the fingers, combining the results. The thumb tends to function as a modifier. For instance, a square thumb will temper the idealistic nature of a pointed first finger.

THE THUMB

The thumb is one of the most important indicators of a person's temperament. Many palmists give the thumb as much significance as all the other fingers combined, and some Hindu practitioners base their entire reading on the thumb alone.

The thumb is divided into three parts, or phalanges. The first phalange, which runs from the tip to the joint, represents willpower. The second phalange, the area from the joint to the palm, is associated with reason. If the first phalange is longer than the second, willpower is stronger. A short second phalange indicates a tactless person with a lack of reasoning power. The third phalange of the thumb is actually part of the palm, known as the mount area of Venus. This area embodies love, affection and sympathy.

An average thumb reaches to the middle of the bottom phalange of first finger. A long thumb is considered more forceful and can strengthen weak lines on the palm. This person is clear-minded and makes a good leader. A very long thumb, however, indicates a tyrant. A short thumb is impressionable and indecisive, often ruled by emotion rather than logic.

A thumb is usually broader than it is thick. A thumb that is as thick as it is broad indicates an unbalanced, perhaps violent, nature, while a slender thumb signifies patience. A 'waisted' thumb—when the second phalange is narrower than first—points to an understanding of both people and animals. A knotty joint on the thumb suggests an analytical mind, whereas a smooth joint betokens an impulsive nature.

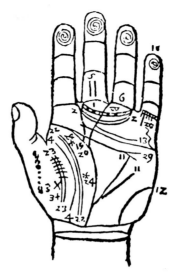

THE FINGERS

Each finger is considered an extension of the mount directly below it and modifies the quality of the mount, with short fingers decreasing the value and long fingers increasing the value. Very long fingers may exaggerate. The overall appearance of the finger is also significant.

The **first finger**—the index or forefinger—is the most important. Known as the finger of Jupiter, it represents ambition. If the top of the first finger is level with the bottom of the nail on the second finger, the person has the ability to be a leader. If the finger is the same length or longer than the second finger, the person is self-centered and a dictator determined to make people obey. If the top of the finger is below the bottom of the nail on the second finger, the person has a tendency to be timid and avoid responsibility.

An index finger that curves toward the second finger indicates acquisitiveness, which can range from simply collecting things to hoarding possessions in a miserly fashion. If only the top phalange curves toward the second finger, the person has a tendency to be stubborn and persistent.

If the first finger is a normal length and shorter than the third finger, the person is a good organizer and is capable of taking charge, but prefers to work with a partner. If the finger is the same length

Above: An illustration from a book on palmistry published in the seventeenth century that is believed to be the first reference to the patterns found on fingerprints.

Below: Types of thumbs, from left to right: stiff-smooth, clubbed, supple-jointed, waisted, knotty-jointed and thick.

as the third finger, the person is well balanced, but if it is longer, the person is proud and desirous of power.

A long and smooth first finger signifies good prospects professionally and socially. A short finger indicates a lack of confidence and stamina, while an extremely short finger indicates a person afraid of the outside world.

A thick first finger suggests a dogged and determined individual. A thin finger indicates an imaginative but unrealistic individual. A crooked finger signifies a crooked person. Finally, if the phalanges are marked with deep, straight, vertical lines, the person is overworked and fatigued.

The **second, or middle, finger** represents Saturn, and if it is strong denotes a melancholy and serious temperament. A straight middle finger, in good proportion to the rest of the fingers, denotes a sensible individual, able to concentrate and plan ahead. A long, strong and heavy middle finger suggests a serious and thoughtful person and one who is likely to have a hard life.

If the finger is the same length as the first and third fingers, the person is immature. A finger that is slightly longer than the first and third fingers indicates an irresponsible person, while a very long finger reveals a morbid and melancholy person. A short middle finger belongs to an intuitive individual. If the middle phalange is the longest, the person loves the country and is said to be 'green-fingered.'

If the middle finger curves, it takes on the qualities of the finger toward which it is curved. A crooked middle finger signifies a person full of self pity.

The **third, or ring, finger** represents Apollo and the individual's inner concerns. A strong and smooth ring finger indicates an emotionally balanced person, while a smooth finger with smooth joints suggests creativity.

A long third finger indicates a longing for fame. These people do well in show business. A very long finger, however, reveals an introverted individual. A short finger signifies a person lacking in emotional control. If the third phalange is the longest, the individual craves money and luxury.

A third finger that bends toward the second finger indicates a person who is apt to be anxiety-ridden and always on the defensive. If the third and

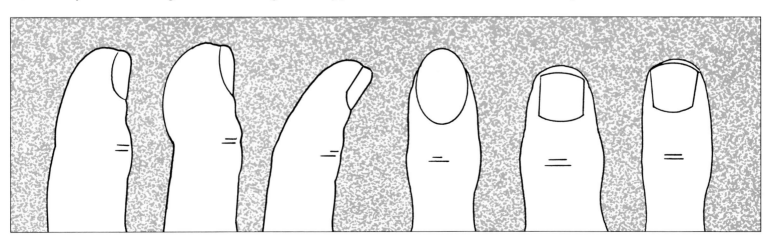

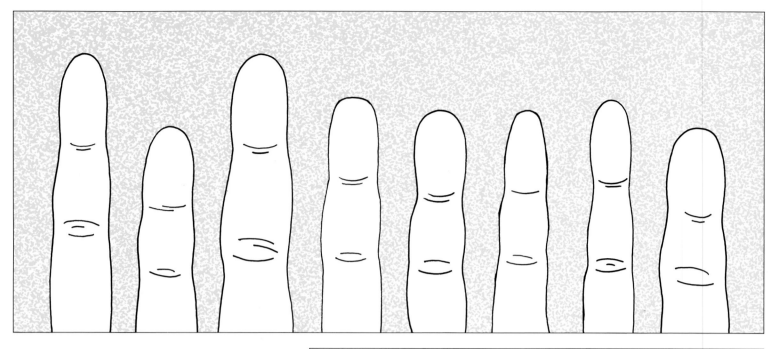

second fingers bend toward each other, the person is secretive. A third finger that droops toward the palm when the hand is relaxed suggests a person who has difficulty dealing with the intuitive aspects of his personality. A crooked or otherwise distorted finger reveals emotional difficulties.

The **fourth, or little, finger** represents Mercury and human relationships. If the fourth finger reaches above the top crease on the third finger, the person is highly intelligent and articulate, but if the finger reaches the nail on the third finger, the individual is untrustworthy. A short fourth finger discloses that the individual has difficulty in making the best of himself.

A long first phalange reveals a knowledgeable person, with an interest in education. However, a first phalange that is considerably longer than the others means the person has a tendency to exaggerate or embellish the truth. A short or almost non-existent third phalange signals a depraved person.

If the fourth finger bends toward the third finger, the person is shrewd and clever in business. If the finger bends toward the palm when the hand is relaxed, the person has sexual difficulties. A twisted or crooked little finger denotes a liar, someone not to be trusted.

Palmists also look at the set of the hand—how the fingers join the hand. For a square hand, the normal set is a straight line across the palm. For all other types of hands, the normal set is a gentle curve, with the first finger set a little lower than the second and third fingers and the fourth finger set slightly lower. A finger that is set noticeably low detracts from the value of the mount.

An additional consideration is the span of the hand, or the distance between the fingers. If the fingers are held together stiffly, the person is likely to be cautious, suspicious and unsociable. If the fingers are evenly spaced, the person has a well-balanced mind and is capable of succeeding in any field. Well-separated fingers indicate an indepen-

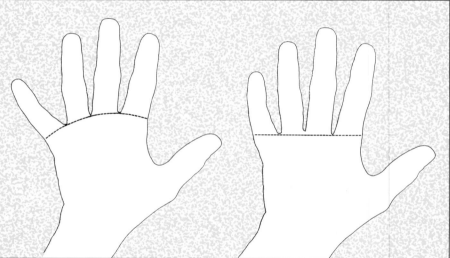

At top: Types of fingers, from left to right: long, short, large, square, spatulate, tapered, slender, and thick and short.

Above: The set of the fingers adds to the interpretation. An individual with fingers set straight across (**right**) tends to be practical and have a positive outlook. An uneven set (**left**) is the most common and indicates that the person must endure life's ups and downs.

Opposite page: The handprint of William Ewart Gladstone, British statesman and orator.

dent and freedom-loving nature. A wide gap between all fingers reveals an open and trusting, almost childlike, disposition.

If the widest space is between the thumb and the first finger, the person has a tendency to be outgoing and generous. If the widest space is between the first and second fingers, the person is not easily influenced by others. If the widest space is between the second and third fingers, the person is light-hearted and anxiety-free. If the widest space is between the third and fourth fingers, the person is an independent and original thinker. If the fourth finger is set far apart from the other fingers, the person is apt to have difficulties in personal relationships and feel isolated and alienated.

The joints add to the meaning of the fingers. Smooth joints reveal an impulsive nature, while knotty joints suggest a deep thinker. Large joints typify a methodical, rational individual.

A pointed fingertip adds idealism; a square tip, practicality; and a spatulate tip, action.

The palmist bases the reading on the total picture. Thus, a square finger with smooth joints is

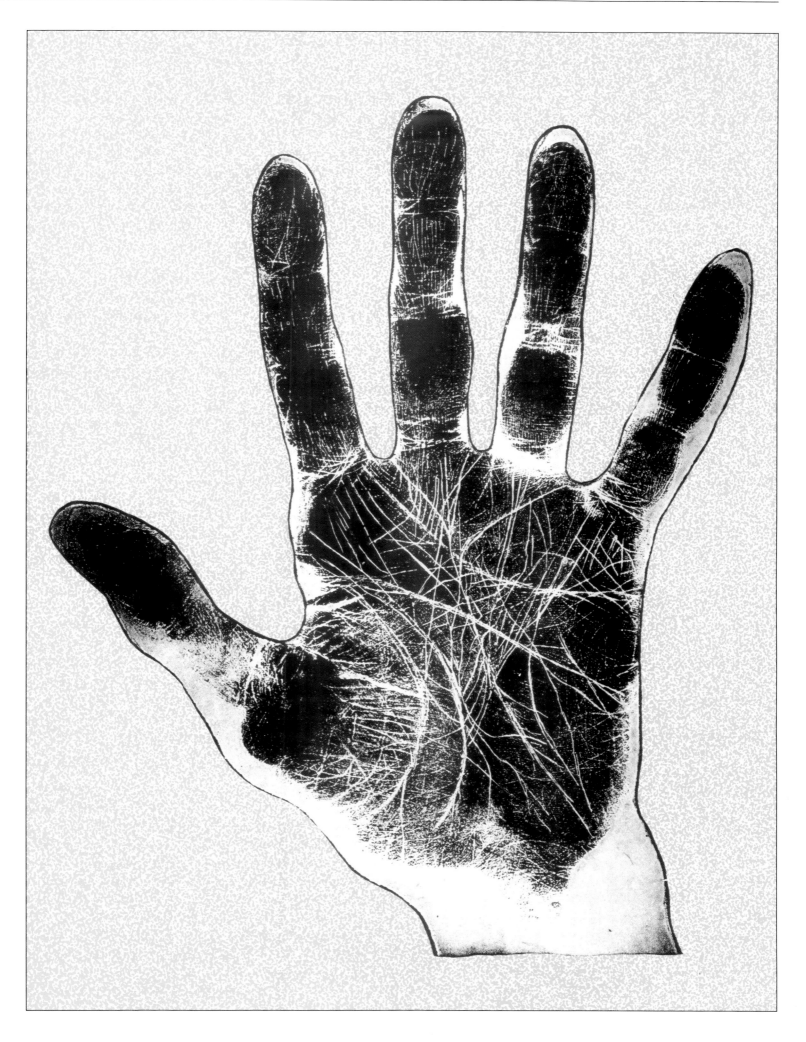

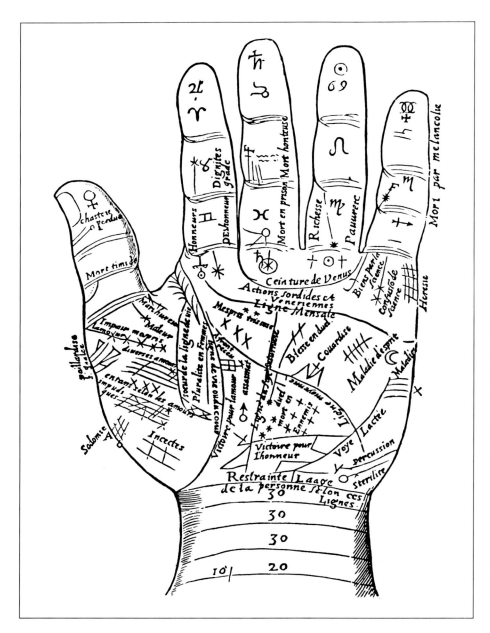

influenced by the practicality indicated by the square shape and the impulsiveness betokened by the smooth joints.

Above: *A chart of Napoleon's hand. Both he and his wife, Josephine, were fervent believers in the science of palmistry.*

THE MOUNTS OF THE PALM

The palm is divided into sections called mounts. Beginning below the first finger the mounts are as follows: Jupiter; Saturn, under the second finger; Apollo, under the third finger; Mercury, under the fourth finger; Upper Mars, below Mercury; Luna (also called the mount of the moon), beneath Upper Mars; Venus, at the base of the thumb (this area is technically the third phalange of the thumb); and Lower Mars, above Venus. The area at the center of the palm is called the Plain of Mars.

The mounts are the keys to an individual's traits and abilities. The higher the mount or the more space it takes, the greater the significance of the area.

The mount of Jupiter symbolizes ambition and social prestige. If the mount is more developed near the side of the palm, family pride drives the individual, but if the development is closer to the head line, the desire to lead is the primary motivator, but the individual should guard against arrogance. If the mount is more developed closer to Saturn, the individual is driven by the pursuit of knowledge.

The **mount of Saturn** is seldom highly developed and is usually influenced by either Jupiter or Apollo or both. Saturn's characteristics are caution and reserve. If the mount is developed closer to the heart line, those characteristics are intensified. If the mount is developed toward Jupiter, the person tends to have a serious outlook on life, but if development is toward Apollo, interest in the arts exerts a strong influence.

The **mount of Apollo** is connected with the arts and signifies brilliance in any field of endeavor. If the mount is developed toward Saturn, a seriousness is added, while development toward Mercury adds a practical, businesslike mind to the artistic talents. An overdeveloped mount suggests a tendency to overrate one's abilities.

The **mount of Mercury** represents hope and typically combines cheerfulness with practicality. The influence of Mercury is seen in a wide range of people, from top level business executives to housewives, for the qualities of Mercury are needed to succeed. If the mount is developed toward Apollo, the person possesses a love of all things beautiful and artistic, and if developed toward the percussion (the side of the palm), a sense of humor is evident. If the mount is developed toward Upper Mars, the person will vigorously support a cause. People of this sort are utterly reliable. An overdeveloped mount can work both positively and negatively, supplying the initiative for inventive minds and successful salespeople but also for criminals and swindlers.

The **mount of Luna** represents imagination, intuition, creative ability and motivation. This is a large area and can vary in form, from bulging all over or in just a few places to thin and almost flat. When the mount is developed toward Upper Mars, the person has the ability to turn dreams into reality. If the percussion bulges, there is the need for physical activity combined with creativity. If development is near the wrist, the person is sensual or imaginative, and if near Venus, romantic and emotional. Development near the Plain of Mars indicates an aggressive nature.

These characteristics are intensified if the mount has a reddish color. A bluish cast reflects a blue, or melancholy, nature. A pale color tends to lessen the effects listed above.

The **mount of Venus** represents love, sympathy, passion and vitality. All of these characteristics come into play if the area is evenly padded and centered. If the mount is developed toward Lower Mars, the person is antagonistic, but if it is developed near the base of the thumb the person is likely to be highly emotional. Development near the wrist indicates an affectionate, sensual nature, while development near Luna reveals self-indulgence.

A low, flat mount indicates a cool, dispassionate nature, while a highly cushioned one reveals a person dynamic in love and friendship. If the area is hard and muscular, the person is resentful.

The **mount of Lower Mars** represents the will to fight for a cause, be it for family, country or self. The action can be either mental or physical. An over-developed mount indicates an abusive temperament, while an underdeveloped area reveals a fearful, reticent individual.

The **mount of Upper Mars** represents endurance, bravery and fortitude. These characteristics signify moral courage rather than physical courage, and complement the action that is the hallmark of Lower Mars. If development of the mount is high or stronger near Mercury, there is no stopping this person, but if the development is near the Plain of Mars, the tendency is to become overly aggressive. Development toward Luna reveals the potential to inspire others, while development toward the percussion suggests a physically reserved individual. An overdeveloped mount means cruelty, while underdeveloped signifies a morbid person.

The **Plain of Mars**, the area in the center of the palm, is influenced by the mounts of Lower and Upper Mars. A high plain indicates good control of one's emotions, especially in arguments, while a flat plain reveals a restrained individual who holds a negative attitude about the world in general.

THE MAJOR LINES

The three major lines—the head, heart and life—are found on almost every palm.

The **life line** represents a person's life energy and vitality. The line begins halfway between the thumb and forefinger and curves around the thumb, ending at or near the wrist. The life line indicates the length of one's life. If the line begins high, near the forefinger, the person is ambitious and not easily deterred. If it starts at the head line, it reveals someone who exhibits an average degree of organization and control, albeit with a measure of caution.

A slight degree of separation between the life and head lines indicates an energetic person capable of succeeding in any walk of life, while a large separation symbolizes an impulsive, uncontrolled person. The gap between the life and head lines also is a good indicator of independence. The wider the gap and the earlier it starts, the greater the tendency to be independent.

Lines that branch upward and end under the first finger show a desire for wealth and power. Lines that drop down toward the thumb indicate a strong need for love and affection.

When the life line ends in the mount of Luna rather than near the thumb, the person requires

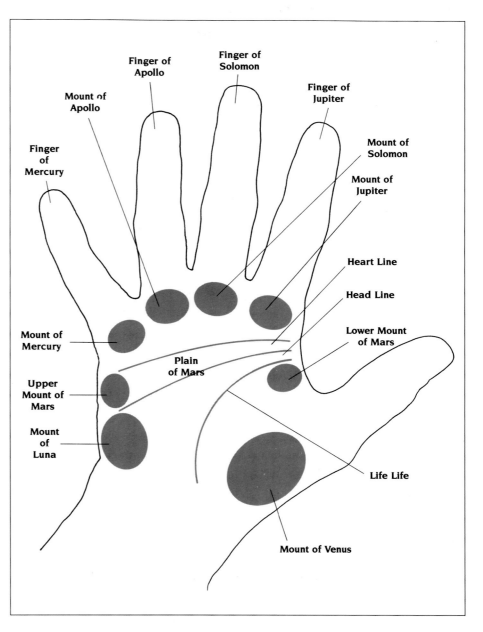

change, such as travel, new surroundings or a variety of occupations.

A branch line extending to the mount of Jupiter, under the first finger, portends great success, either in business or marriage.

A line to Saturn, under the second finger, signifies a deeply religious person, often with a strong need for solitude.

A line to Apollo, under the third finger, reveals wealth or fame. If the line is straight, wealth is achieved with the help of family or friends. If wavy or broken, the path to fame and fortune will be filled with obstacles.

A strong, connecting line to Mercury denotes prosperity in business, usually with the assistance of loved ones.

A line to Upper Mars suggests unusual bravery or physical strength.

Small lines that intersect the life line are interpreted as situations that hinder business or cause unhappiness in one's personal life. Those lines that radiate from the thumb and go through the life line show a tendency to be easily influenced by family and friends.

The **head line** is associated with mental attitudes—the level of intelligence, breadth of understanding and use of one's intellectual potential. The longer the line, the greater the importance of intellectual concerns.

This line starts near or at the same place as the life line, about midway between the thumb and forefinger, and crosses the palm toward the outside of the hand.

If the head line is joined to the life line, it reveals a cautious nature. The longer the two lines are joined, the greater the caution. Being joined a long time also shows being close to or dependent on one's family for a long time.

A separation between the two lines shows a desire to forge ahead, but if the separation is great, this becomes a restless, headlong quality.

A line that goes across the palm, gently sloping to the area between Upper Mars and Luna is considered the average head line and indicates a good intellect and a practical nature. The line typically extends to Apollo or Mercury but not to the edge of the hand.

A long and straight line reveals a shrewd individual with a good memory.

A line that slopes toward the mount of Luna belongs to a person who is sensitive and imaginative. If the line slopes even further and ends at the top part of Luna, the person has a talent for self-expression, but if it ends at the lower part of Luna, the imagination is over-active. A line that ends at the lower part of Luna can even indicate madness.

Below: The art of divination, or foretelling the future, is practiced all over the world. Signs such as this one advertising palm reading can be found in cities, towns and villages throughout the world.

If the line runs toward the center of the wrist, the individual is out of touch with reality.

A line that curves upward to the heart line reveals an aptitude for business and the ability to make money, but a line that runs close to the heart line suggests a narrow outlook on life.

A clear, firm line denotes common sense, while a thin, light line signifies indecision. A red line reveals an aggressive nature. A short line means that the person will need assistance to achieve success, while a very short line indicates insufficient ambition or energy to complete one's goals.

A head line that ends under Saturn portends low intelligence, insanity or premature death if there are other indicators of poor health.

If the line ends under Apollo, the individual is light-hearted and cheerful and often succeeds in the arts. Persons of this sort generally desire the easy path to wealth.

If the line ends under Mercury, the person will make an excellent manager in any field.

A forked ending pointing to Luna shows imagination that is restrained by common sense, but a fork that ends on the heart line reveals a person willing to sacrifice all for the sake of all.

A strong branch line stemming from the head line to Jupiter indicates high ambitions that lead to success.

A heavy branch line to Saturn expresses religious fervor.

A branch to Apollo signals the ability to attain success through one's talents.

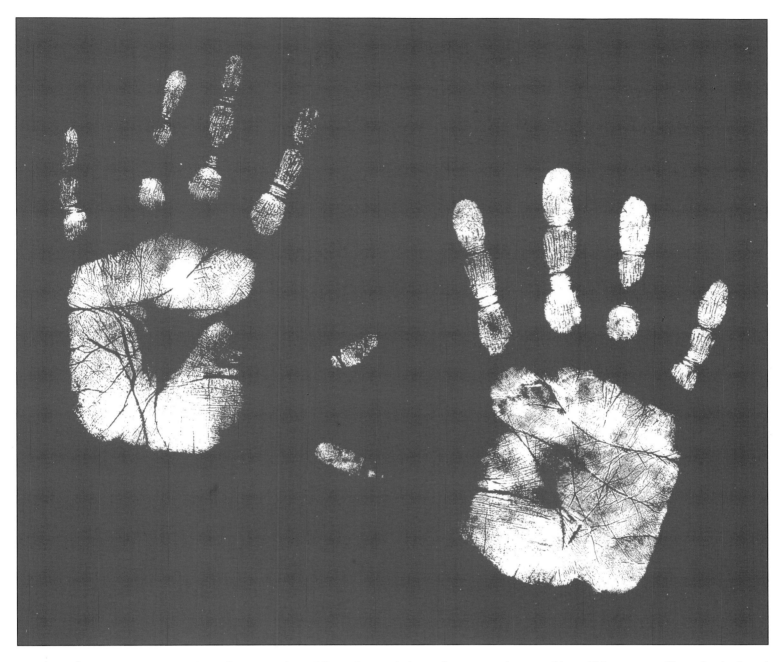

A branch to Mercury is a sign of success in business.

A branch line to the mount of Luna area is usually indicative of an active imagination, but the final analysis is dependent on the reading of the total hand.

The **heart line** represents the emotional and physical traits associated with the heart. The first horizontal line on the palm, the heart line usually starts in the mount of Jupiter and runs across the palm at the base of the mounts to the opposite edge.

A heart line that starts high, almost at the base of the forefinger, signals a jealous person, while a line that starts low and runs in a straight line indicates affection for family but with little show of emotion.

A line that starts between the first and second fingers reveals sensual love, a tolerant nature and a generous attitude.

A line that starts between the second and third fingers belongs to a person with a negative atti-

Above: *Some palmists prefer to do a reading from a handprint rather than from the hand itself.*

tude toward love. This person will need to be loved by an understanding individual.

If the heart line drops down and joins the head line, the head is said to rule the heart.

If the heart, head and life lines all start at the same point, the person is an extremist unwilling to use good judgment.

If the heart line starts in a fork on the mount of Jupiter, the individual is lovable and makes a good marriage partner. However, if one prong of the fork lies on Jupiter and the other on Saturn, the person is apt to be moody and difficult to live with.

A double heart line indicates an increased capacity for love and affection, whereas a missing line means a selfish person.

A branch line that runs to the head line indicates an attachment formed at work or a married couple that works together.

A branch line to the life line expresses sorrow over the loss of a loved one.

A branch line to Mercury indicates the collapse of a business due to family or a loved one.

The Ouija Board's Messages from Beyond

☾☾☾☾☾

T here is a story, sworn true by a college professor at a prestigious American university, of a Ouija board whose warnings were not heeded, with tragic results for a group of friends.

Upon the death of his grandmother, this college professor inherited an old house in the Gothic and mysterious city of New Orleans. The house was full of his grandmother's belongings, all left in her will to her sole grandchild. She made only one stipulation: her grandson was not to open a certain trunk in the attic under any circumstances. Figuring the trunk held old love letters or some other private belongings, he respected her wishes. Also, he was not a very curious man.

In the true spirit of a Crescent City denizen, the college professor had a week-long party in his new home, inviting all his best friends from his own college days. The friends drank wine, and explored all corners of the big old house. The women began trying on all the old dresses they found, opening bureaus, armoires, and finally, the trunk up in the attic. There they found a Ouija board under dusty petticoats and faded hoop-skirts. There was a note

in an old-fashioned hand, which read:

'If you choose to play with things of evil,
You will have your day with the devil.'

The women brought the board downstairs, lit some candles, and held a mock séance. The professor started to protest the opening of the trunk, but he didn't want his friends to think he was superstitious. So he said nothing.

The friends asked the board how and when they would die. For each of them, the board spelled out a horrible fate: burnings, stabbings, car accidents, drownings. They laughed, though some looked nervous and had a little more wine.

The woman who knocked the rusty lock off the trunk was the first to die. That very night, she fell from the widow's walk down to the rose garden. People said she had drunk too much wine, but amongst themselves the friends whispered of the truth in the board's omen for her: 'Fall.'

One by one, the Ouija board's prophecies came true. Some tried to escape their fate as foretold by the old woman's board. A few moved to foreign countries, another changed her name. But only one of the friends survived: the college professor. When he had asked his future of his dead grandmother's board that fateful night, the one word reply was this: 'Remember.'

FROM THE BEGINNING TO THE PRESENT

For many people, the Ouija board has a connotation of slumber party séances, but it can be a channel for communication with spirits or other energies, or for the unleashing of subconscious thoughts and desires. The typical divination board is a thin sheet of wood approximately 18 inches by 12 inches. Printed on the board are the numbers 0-9, the letters A-Z, and the words, 'Yes,' 'No' and 'Maybe.' The boards are usually waxed or varnished to provide a smooth gliding surface for the pointer, or planchette.

The origins of the Ouija board are ancient and arise from many different cultures. Analogous boards are known to have existed in China in 800 BC. Pythagoras wrote about divination boards in Greece around 540 BC. In thirteenth century Tartary, the Mongols used boards akin to Ouija boards to prepare their battle strategies. Native Americans used boards they called *squdilatc* to locate lost articles and missing persons, and to decide how and when religious ceremonies should be performed.

The Ouija board is set on a level, steady surface. The participants, usually only one or two people, may seek communication with spirits of the dead, or they may simply direct a question to the board. The most commonly asked questions are about love, work and death. The fingertips of the partici-

Previous page: *With fingertips lightly resting on the planchette, a seeker questions the board.*

Above: *The modern planchette closely resembles the original instrument, whose invention in 1853 by the French spiritualist M Planchette spurred the divination board into great popularity.*

pants are placed on or near the pointer, but never consciously manipulate it in any way. According to most theories, the planchette is moved across the board by the energies emanating from the tips of the fingers, or by muscle impulses originating in the subconscious. The message is spelled out when the pointer hovers over a letter or number. If these energies are shaped by the subconscious thoughts of the participants, the Ouija board provides a roadmap of their inner thinking.

In 1853, the boards became a huge fad throughout Europe when a French spiritualist named M Planchette invented an instrument for use on divination boards. The design was similar to that of the pointer that Parker Bros now manufactures. Triangular in shape, the 'planchette' has three legs, one of which is a pencil.

It wasn't until 38 years later that the board was patented. In 1891, Elijah J Bond received a US patent, then sold the rights a year later to William Fuld, who was issued another patent for the board. Fuld founded the Southern Novelty Co in Baltimore, Maryland, later changing the name to the Baltimore Talking Board Company, and began producing Oriole Talking Boards. Fuld consulted the board for advice on building the factory, but proclaimed, 'I'm no spiritualist. I'm a Presbyterian.' He asserted that he never used the board himself after the completion of the factory.

In 1920, Fuld went to court to fight the taxable status of Ouija boards, arguing that they were not games, but spiritual tools, and therefore should be exempt from taxation. The court ruled against him, conceding that the Talking Boards were not ordinary games, but that they would commonly be used as such.

In 1966, Parker Bros bought the Baltimore Talking Board Company. Ironically, they moved the factory to Salem, Massachusetts, the scene of the infamous seventeenth century witch trials. They sold over two million Ouija boards that year, outselling their perennial best-seller, Monopoly.

COMMUNICATION WITH THE SPIRIT WORLD

The popularity of the Talking Boards soars during times of crisis. During war time, the friends and family of the soldiers seek answers about the well-being of their loved ones, or try to communicate with those who have been killed. The boards also sell well in times of nationwide financial straits, such as the Great Depression, or political and social upheaval, like the '60s.

Messages have been known to appear in code or in languages unknown by the participants, later being decoded or translated to reveal what would seem to be a communication from beyond.

There are many stories of Ouija boards which were beneficial to their users. In 1937, Mrs Pearl Curran was using her Ouija board with her sister, when suddenly the spirit of a dead woman introduced herself through the board. The woman, whose name had been Patience Worth, began to dictate her writings to Pearl by spelling out the words on the Ouija board.

Patience, through Pearl's transcription, produced over 2500 poems, many of which were published in Braithwaite's Anthology of Poetry, an annual compendium of the best poems of the year. Patience also produced a full-length play, called Redwing, and dictated five best-selling historical novels, full of rich period detail. The Sorry Tale, the story of Jesus Christ's earthly life, was 300,000 words long and took Pearl over two years to transcribe. Eventually, public interest in Patience

waned. Pearl had grown older and less able to keep up with Patience's exhausting literary output. After Pearl's death in 1952, Patience was never heard from again.

Many Ouija practitioners have served as spiritual secretaries. A particular married couple, both writers, often approach their board with questions concerning their craft, as well as other aspects of their lives. They have transcribed thousands of pages from their Ouija board, some of which they've assimilated into their own writing projects.

Some spiritualists warn, however, that the entities which speak through the board may not be the benevolent loved ones who have passed away, but instead, evil spirits and demons. In 1935, Mrs Nellie Hurd of Kansas City, Missouri, was told by a Ouija board that her husband had given $15,000 to a woman who, according to the board, was his mistress. Mr Hurd could not convince his wife of his innocence, because the Ouija board kept contradicting him. Mrs Hurd began to lose her sanity, and to beat, burn and torture her husband, who eventually killed her.

Demonologist Leonard Stephens believes that people using a Ouija board may protect themselves by observing simple precautions. Persons working alone, for long hours or while in a state of anger, can create dangerous apertures between this world and the beyond. Stephens also cautions that certain stages in a one's life make one more susceptible to attack. Middle age and adolescence seem to be the most vulnerable times, perhaps because of the emotional upheavals common to these periods.

The Ouija board may be used safely, but its power must be respected and not taken lightly.

Below: This planchette is indicating the letter 'S'. Some querants have transcribed entire original novels from the words spelled out by their boards.

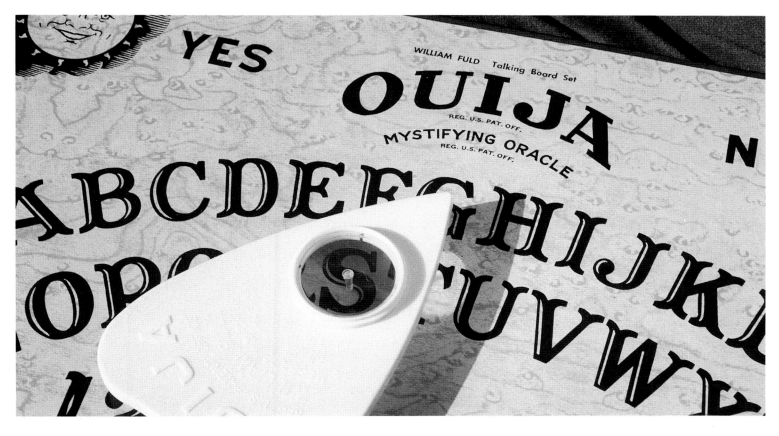

The Exalted Wisdom of the I Ching

The I *Ching* or *Book of Changes* is an ancient and complex system of divination that originated in China during the third millennium BC. However, the I *Ching* is much more than a means of prediction. It is a book of wisdom that offers advise on how to deal with the fortune. The central feature of the I *Ching* is the hexagram, a pattern of six lines read from the bottom upward. The hexagram is formed, or cast, by yarrow stalks, coins or wands. Once the hexagram is formed, the *Book of Changes* is consulted for interpretation and advice.

Fu Hsi, who according to legend was the first emperor of China, is said to be one of the earliest developers of the I *Ching*. Under the Hsia Dynasty (2205-1766 BC) and the Shang Dynasty (1176-1150 BC) two early books of changes were used for divination. In the fifth century BC, the great writer and sage Confucius is believed to have studied and used the I *Ching*, adding a written commentary of his own. He is credited with saying that it has 'as many layers as the earth itself.'

Under the Ch'in (221-206 BC) and Han (206-220

AD) Dynasties the I *Ching* was used solely as a means of divining the future, and lost the Confucian context that held that its higher purpose was to guide ethical statecraft.

The Swiss psychologist and philosopher Carl Gustav Jung took a keen interest in the ancient *Book of Changes*. He was hoping to find a connection between 'this oracle technique, or method of exploring the unconscious' and his synchronicity concept. Jung's fascination with coincidence led him to develop the concept of synchronicity, or the 'simultaneous occurrence of a certain psychic state with one or more external events which appear as meaningful parallels to the momentary subjective state.'

Traditionally, the I *Ching* has been used to encourage deep thought and self-examination. At first, the linear signs were meant to represent the answers yes and no. 'Yes' was indicated by an unbroken line (———) and has become affiliated with Yang, the positive, masculine and active side of nature. 'No' was indicated by a broken line (— —)and is today known as Yin, symbolizing the negative, feminine and passive side of nature. It soon became evident that many questions required more than a simple yes or no answer, and the lines were paired:

Then a third line was added to each of these pairs, thus forming the eight trigrams which are the fundamental tools for forecasting the future.

The eight trigrams represent all that takes place in Heaven and on Earth. They symbolize the transitional nature of processes in the physical world instead of representing an entity in a fixed state. This relates to the widely-held belief that what occurs in the visible world is merely the effect of an 'image' or idea in the unseen world. Change is not without meaning and the *Book of Changes* is a record of all the complex, interconnected changes, such as night and day.

The trigrams also represent a family unit consisting of a father, mother, three sons and three daughters. Generally, the sons are associated with movement—beginning of movement, danger in movement, rest and completion of movement—while the daughters are associated with devotion—gentle penetration, clarity and adaptability, and joyous tranquility. However, some practitioners find other themes in the trigrams, such as animals, body parts, time of day and points of a compass.

Each trigram is assigned an attribute—a word or so that describes the potential action in a given combination of lines—and an image of Heaven, Earth or a feature of one of the two. The image gives added meaning to the interpretation of the trigram.

THE EIGHT TRIGRAMS OF THE I CHING

Name	Image	Attribute	Relationship
Ch'ien, The Creative	Heaven	strong	father
K'un, The Receptive	Earth	devoted, yielding	mother
Chen, The Arousing	Thunder	inciting movement	first son
K'an, The Abysmal	Water	dangerous	second son
K'en, Keeping Still	Mountain	resting	third son
Sun, The Gentle	Wind	penetrating	first daughter
Li, The Clinging	Fire	light-giving	second daughter
Tui, The Joyous	Lake	joyful	third daughter

THE ANCIENT BEAUTY OF THE 64 HEXAGRAMS

The eight triagrams were combined with each other in every possible configuration, and the resulting 64 hexagrams today make up the entire *Book of Changes* as expounded by King Wen.

Below are the names of the 64 hexagrams in the order that they appear in the I *Ching*.

1	Ch'ien	The Creative
2	K'un	The Receptive
3	Chun	Difficulty at the Beginning
4	Meng	Youthful Folly
5	Hsu	Waiting (Nourishment)
6	Sung	Conflict
7	Shih	The Army
8	Pi	Holding Together
9	Hsiao Ch'u	The Taming Power of the Small
10	Lu	Treading
11	T'ai	Peace
12	P'i	Standstill
13	T'ung Jen	Fellowship with Men
14	Ta Yu	Possession in Great Measure
15	Ch'ien	Modesty
16	Yu	Enthusiasm
17	Sui	Following
18	Ku	Work on What Has Been Spoiled
19	Lin	Approach
20	Kuan	Contemplation (View)
21	Shih Ho	Biting Through
22	Pi	Grace
23	Po	Splitting Apart
24	Fu	Return (The Turning Point)
25	Wu Wang	Innocence (The Unexpected)
26	Ta Ch'u	The Taming Power of the Great
27	I	The Corners of the Mouth (Providing Nourishment)
28	Ta Kuo	Preponderance of the Great
29	K'an	The Abysmal (Water)
30	Li	The Clinging, Fire
31	Hsien	Influence (Wooing)
32	Heng	Duration
33	Tun	Retreat
34	Ta Chuang	The Power of the Great
35	Chin	Progress
36	Ming I	Darkening of the Light
37	Chia Jen	The Family
38	K'uei	Opposition
39	Chien	Obstruction
40	Hsieh	Deliverance
41	Sun	Decrease
42	I	Increase
43	Kuai	Breakthrough (Resoluteness)
44	Kou	Coming to Meet
45	Ts'ui	Gathering Together
46	Sheng	Pushing Upward
47	K'un	Oppression (Exhaustion)
48	Ching	The Well
49	Ko	Revolution (Molting)

Page 39: These Chinese bronze coins are the preferred type of coin to use when forming an I Ching hexagram, but any two-sided coin will work.

Opposite page: From a hanging scroll dated 1707 AD. The hexagram of K'un, The Receptive, is associated with the Earth.

Above: An eighteenth-century Chinese illustration showing the eight trigrams that make up the 64 hexagrams of the I Ching.

Right: The throwing of the yarrow stalks is a revered tradition, as illustrated by this ancient scroll.

50	Ting	The Cauldron
51	Chen	The Arousing (Shock, Thunder)
52	K'en	Keeping Still
53	Chien	Development (Gradual Progress)
54	Kuei Mei	The Marrying Maiden
55	Feng	Abundance
56	Lu	The Wanderer
57	Sun	The Gentle (The Penetrating, Wind)
58	Tui	The Joyous, Lake
59	Huan	Dispersion
60	Chieh	Limitation
61	Chung Fu	Inner Truth
62	Hsiao Kuo	Preponderance of the Small
63	Chi Chi	After Completion
64	Wei Chi	Before Completion

FORMING AND READING THE HEXAGRAM

There are two ways to consult the oracle. The first is very ancient and complicated. It requires sorting and separating 50 yarrow stalks derived from the sacred yarrow plant.

Separate one yarrow stalk from the pile. This stalk has no further role. The remaining 49 are divided into two random heaps. From the right-hand pile, take one stalk and place it between the ring finger and the little finger of the left hand. Place the left-hand heap in the left hand and draw stalks from it with the right hand four at a time until there are four or fewer stalks remaining. Place the remainder between the ring finger and the middle finger of the left hand. Divide the right-hand pile by the same method and place the remainder between the middle finger and the fore-finger of the left hand. Now count the stalks between the fingers of the left hand. The sum will

gradually takes shape, built from the bottom line up. Once the hexagram is established, the interpretation can be looked up in the I Ching.

The coin oracle is a much simpler method requiring three coins. Old Chinese bronze coins with an inscription on one side and a square hole in the middle are the preferred type, but any two-sided coin will work. The three coins are tossed together six times. If they land with the inscribed side up, that counts as Yin with a value of two. The reverse side up counts as Yang with a value of three. Each toss determines the character of one line in the hexagram. If all three coins are Yang, then the line is a nine. If all three are Yin, then the line is a six. Two Yin and one Yang give the line a value of seven, and two Yang and one Yin yield an eight. By consulting the I Ching commentaries on the hexagrams, the answer will become evident.

In both methods, the function of 'strong' or 'moving' lines comes into play. A strong Yang line has a circle over the center, while a strong Yin line has a cross in the gap. When strong lines appear, the hexagram is first interpreted according to the commentary in the I Ching, then read again with the strong lines turned into their opposites—strong Yin becomes Yang, while strong Yang becomes Yin. Thus, a new hexagram is formed, and it too is interpreted according to the Book of Changes.

The hexagrams can be read in a variety of ways, each revealing various themes and interpretations. First, the hexagram is read from bottom to top, the bottom line being one and the top six (see below). The odd-numbered lines are superior in value, while the even-numbered lines are inferior. If the hexagram is divided into three pairs (see below), (a) represents the earth, (b) man, and (c) heaven. Another way to read the hexagram is by looking at the bottom three and top three lines. They are referred to as the lower (d) and upper (e) primary trigrams. Finally, the nuclear trigrams are those two trigrams (see below) which are interlocked within the hexagram and bounded by lines one and six. They are the lower (f) and upper (g) nuclear trigrams.

The character of the Yang and Yin lines are by nature positive or negative, 'the firm' and 'the

be either nine or five. Disregard the first stalk held between the little finger and the ring finger. The new total will be one less than before. Four is considered a complete numerical unit and is assigned the value of three. It follows that eight is regarded as a double unit. It is assigned a value of two. If the left-over stalks in the left hand numbered nine at first, their assigned value would be two. If at first they numbered five, their assigned value would be three. The remaining stalks are gathered again and divided as before. This time the remainders will be eight or four, which bear the assigned values of two or three. This procedure is carried out a third time. Again the remainders will be eight or four with assigned values of two or three. The sum of the numerical values of the remainders will determine the character of the line. If it is nine, it is an old Yang. If it is seven, it is a young Yang. If it is eight, it is an old Yin. If it is six, it is a young Yin.

Yang lines are considered positive, while the Yin are negative. The old Yang and old Yin are moving lines and designated by the symbol O. The young Yang and young Yin are at rest and designated by the symbol X. This entire process is repeated six times. Each time adds a line and the hexagram

Above: *The hexagram Ch'ien, The Creative, is represented by the image of Heaven, and is associated with the four attributes of sublimity, potential for success, power to further, and perseverance.*

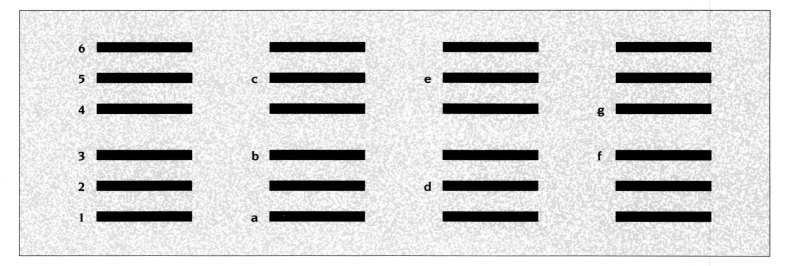

yielding,' but their influence varies according to their relative positions. Reading the hexagrams requires a clear mind and concentration because the text of the I Ching is complex and cryptic, and is best interpreted by an experienced reader.

The text may have up to five sections, depending on the editor. The judgment, the essence of the hexagram, is a brief poem of sorts composed by King Wen. The commentary on the judgment is self-explanatory and originated with Confucius or during a later period. The image (or symbol) is also attributed to King Wen. The image makes the judgment easier to understand by associating King Wen's cryptic words with imagery from the physical world. The lines are interpretations of the moving lines by King Wen's son, the Duke of Chou. This section of the text offers more direct advice than the other sections do. Some editors include other commentaries that add clarifying remarks to the older parts of the text. These remarks may well show the influence of a particular point of view, such as Jungian psychology.

Below are the eight double trigrams and a brief explanation of their meanings.

1 Ch'ien, The Creative

————— upper Ch'ien, The Creative, Heaven
—————
—————
————— lower Ch'ien, The Creative, Heaven
—————
—————

Below: The image of the Earth is associated with the hexagram K'un, the Receptive, which brings about sublime success through quiet perseverance.

The Judgment: The Creative works sublime success, furthering through perseverance.

This hexagram is the symbol of the fourth month in the Chinese calendar. Associated with this hexagram are the four attributes of sublimity, potential for success, power to further, and perseverance. Whoever draws this oracle will gain success from the primal forces of the universe, and by persevering in what is right, happiness will come to them and others.

The double image of Heaven represented by the trigram Ch'ien in the upper and lower position symbolizes the unending course of time. The aspect of time is inherent in the power of the first hexagram. The sign of Heaven is the circle and the color is midnight blue.

The Duke of Chou's interpretation of the lines focuses on the dragon. The dragon symbolizes a dynamic, creative force that is electrically charged and manifests itself in the thunderstorm. The early summer is the time when this arousing force is active, and the light-giving power activates the Earth's creative forces. During the winter the energy withdraws into the Earth.

2 K'un, The Receptive

— — upper K'un, The Receptive, Earth
— —
— —
— — lower K'un, The Receptive, Earth
— —
— —

Above: *Keeping Still, or Ken, is represented by a mountain. A person who can maintain the sort of stillness and solidity of a mountain can achieve great things.*

Left: *The Chinese often illustrated their texts with beautiful ink drawings, such as this landscape from the early Ch'ing Dynasty, which is dated 1661 AD.*

Opposite page: *Water, in the I Ching as in many other systems, symbolizes life-giving properties.*

The Judgment: The Receptive brings about sublime success, furthered through the perseverance of a mare. If the superior man undertakes something and tries to lead, he goes astray; but if he follows, he finds guidance. It is favorable to find friends in the west and south, to forego friends in the east and north. Quiet perseverance brings good fortune.

The broken lines of K'un represent the dark, yielding, receptive primal power of Yin. The attribute of the Receptive is devotion, and the image is the Earth. It is the perfect complement to the Creative, and shares the four fundamental aspects of 'sublime success furthering through perseverance,' but the Creative is associated with the mare rather than the dragon. While the two hexagrams are opposite in structure, they are not opposite in meaning. Both share the aspect of time because their structure is that of doubled trigrams. However, time for the Receptive is a doubling of the Earth, and this means the Earth carries and preserves all things on it, good or evil.

The sign of the Receptive is the square, a solid, primary form and the symbol of the Earth. Yellow is the Earth's color.

51 Chen, The Arousing

```
— —   upper Chen, The Arousing, Thunder
— —
———
— —   lower Chen, The Arousing, Thunder
— —
———
```

The Judgment: Shock brings success. Shock comes—oh, oh! Laughing words—ha, ha! The shock terrifies for a hundred miles, and he does not let fall the sacrificial spoon and chalice.

This symbol reflects the first son who seizes the throne with energy and power. The shock comes from the violent movement of the Yang line as it presses upward against the two Yin lines. As thunder bursts over the Earth it causes fear and trembling.

It is the spirit of inner seriousness and reverence for God that protects the great ruler from fear. In many cases, the fear caused by this highly charged sign is followed by joy and merriment.

There are three kinds of shock—the shock of Heaven (thunder), the shock of fate, and the shock of the heart.

29 K'an, The Abysmal

— — upper K'an, The Abysmal, Water
— —
— — lower K'an, The Abysmal, Water
———
— —

The Judgment: The Abysmal repeated. If you are sincere, you have success in your heart, and whatever you do succeeds.

K'an means a plunging in, and it is illustrated in the hexagram by a Yang line that has plunged in between two Yin lines. The Yang line is bounded by the two Yin lines just like water in a ravine. This hexagram symbolizes the middle son in the family relationships of the eight double trigrams, and as such shares characteristics with the Creative and the Receptive. From the Creative above comes the life-giving property of water, and as it flows on the Receptive Earth it brings new life.

'The Abysmal repeated' refers to danger, which if repeatedly encountered can teach a person to rely on inner strength and virtue. On the contrary, by growing used to that which is dangerous, a person can let evil become a part of them, and misfortune will be the result.

52 Ken, Keeping Still

——— upper Ken, Keeping Still, Mountain
— —
— —
——— lower Ken, Keeping Still, Mountain
— —
— —

The Judgment: Keeping Still. Keeping his back still so that he no longer feels his body. He goes into his courtyard and does not see his people. No blame.

This hexagram signifies the end and beginning of all movement, the moment of resting. Whoever acts from this deep level of inner harmony and harmony with the universe makes no mistakes. For

example, a heart at rest leads to the complete elimination of egotistic drives and leaves a person free to concern themselves with loftier pursuits.

57 Sun, The Gentle

——— upper Sun, The Gentle, Wind
———
— —
——— lower Sun, The Gentle, Wind
———
— —

The Judgment: The Gentle. Success through what is small. It furthers one to have somewhere to go. It furthers one to see the great man.

This is the symbol of the eldest daughter, whose image is wind or wood. Its attribute is 'penetrating'; this oracle signifies the power of light penetrating darkness, of wind clearing the sky of clouds, of incisive judgment that foils all hidden motives. It can also portend the influence of a powerful personality who will uncover and dissolve conspiracies in a community.

Change is inherent in Sun, as in all the hexagrams. However, change should be effected through gentle influence that never lapses rather than through violent means. The oracle of this hexagram encourages deliberation before action, but cautions against repeated questioning or 'penetration,' which will surely bring humiliation on a leader for showing indecision.

30 Li, The Clinging

——— upper Li, The Clinging, Fire
— —
———
——— lower Li, The Clinging, Fire
— —
———

The Judgment: The Clinging. Perseverance furthers. It brings success. Care of the cow brings good fortune.

As a dark Yin line clings to two light Yang lines, the empty space makes the strong lines appear bright. Each of the two trigrams represent the sun. Doubled they represent the repeated movement of the sun and the function of light with respect to time. The ceaseless passage of time reflected in this hexagram reminds human beings that their lives are transitory and conditional.

The cow exemplifies extreme docility. In relation to finding one's place in the world, Li urges cultivating an attitude of compliance in order to develop clarity without sharpness. In the theme of the family, Li is the second daughter.

58 Tui, The Joyous

— — upper Tui, The Joyous, Lake
———
———
— — lower Tui, The Joyous, Lake
———
———

The Judgment: The Joyous. Success. Perseverance is favorable.

This double trigram denotes the youngest daughter and is symbolized by the smiling lake. Its attribute is joyousness, indicated by the two strong lines within expressing themselves through the gentleness of the Yin line above. Tui imparts that true joy that comes from within and must be based on steadfastness, outwardly gentle and inwardly firm.

Tui is the image of a lake which rejoices and refreshes all living things.

__Right:__ This image is drawn from hexagram 41, mountain above, lake below.

The Uncanny Power of Coffee Grounds and Tea Leaves

A young man, bored and restless, was working behind the counter of his parents' café in Athens, Georgia. He was cursing them under his breath for trapping him in this 'den of ethnicity,' as he called it. The café's floor and couches were blanketed with satin-covered pillows, the lamps dripped long silk tassels, and the smell of incense mixed with the smells of coffee and curried food. But he had to continue to work there to help meet his tuition at the local university. He was studying for his degree in Business Administration.

A young girl entered the Greek café on this rainy, cold winter day. She ordered some Turkish coffee and sat by the window to watch the rain come down. The young man behind the counter asked her if she would like to have her fortune read.

The girl gave him a disdainful smile, and shook her head. 'No, thanks,' she said. 'I don't believe in that kind of superstitious garbage.' She pulled one

of her college textbooks, *Introduction to Psychology*, from her knapsack and began to read.

'Garbage! This is handed down from my great-grandmother, a wise woman, who learned it at the knee of *her* great-grandmother.' The young man affected a slight foreign accent—just what kind it was supposed to be, he wasn't sure.

'There is no reason why my coffee grounds would predict my future. Besides, don't you believe in free will?'

'Oh, you are a modern girl, one who needs proof, and science and explanations. Well, I am a Gypsy,' he lied, 'and some things we know without seeing. And without someone else telling us in long words, we know what we see.' He tapped her textbook, stared at her for a moment and then walked behind a red curtain into the back room.

The girl sat at the table blushing. She closed her textbook, walked over to the curtain and called to him, 'Please, read my fortune for me.'

'Perhaps,' was his only response.

Behind the red curtain, the young man carefully prepared the cup that he would use to read her fortune. He worked very quickly, sprinkling used coffee grounds over the design he had laid out in glue. Leaving the cup in the back room to dry, he approached the table near the window. He inspected the cup from which the girl had been drinking and declared it unfit for a reading—too little of the coffee was left. He offered to prepare her another cup for the reading.

Keeping a wary eye on the girl, he dashed into the back and grabbed the specially treated cup. He prepared a fresh batch of Turkish coffee. Just before pouring the coffee in, he tested the glue. The heart he had made on the bottom of the cup was dry.

He and the girl talked as she slowly sipped the coffee, and he waited nervously for her to finish her coffee and see his message for her there.

'There,' she said, replacing the cup in the saucer. She seemed nervous as well.

He turned the cup upside-down and waited for the thick syrup to pour out. He had seen his grandmother do this a million times, and had always laughed at her.

After a few moments, he turned the cup over, expecting to find the large heart on the bottom. It was gone. 'The glue must have melted!' he said out loud.

'What *glue*?' asked the girl, narrowing her eyes.

'Nothing,' he said.

Previous page: *The shape of the bell, as seen among the tea leaves in this cup, augurs good news.*

Below, center row, top to bottom: *A crown and a mushroom, as they might appear when formed by tea leaves in a tea cup. Once decoded, these symbols offer information, warnings and advice. Perceiving a crown in your cup portends that fortune will bring esteem, and a mushroom counsels that problems must be addressed.*

Bottom row, left to right: *A harp symbolizes romance and happiness; an hourglass warns of potential danger; an angel heralds good news; a pipe signifies the virtue of open-mindedness; and a bell augurs good news, possibly of a wedding. These are just some of the symbols which may appear on the inside of a querant's tea cup.*

The girl picked up the cup and peered inside. 'Well, I see a great big anchor near the top of the cup, and what looks like a bell down near the bottom.'

'I'm supposed to be the Gypsy here,' he said, holding out his hand for the cup.

'*Supposed* to be, is right,' she said, handing him the cup.

'An anchor, I see that, and the bell—I see it, too! Let's go look it up.' She looked puzzled, so he added, 'My grandmother made me a list once when I was little of what to look for.'

The grandmother's list is reproduced here, so the reader may see that the reading produced a much happier fortune than just a charlatan heart which melted away.

On their wedding day, the young man gave his bride the cup, with the anchor and the bell still embossed in an intaglio on the white china.

THE STUDY OF TASSEOGRAPHY

What remains in the bottom of a coffee cup may be more important than what is sipped out of it. These readings cannot be performed with common automatic drip coffee or tea bags, but only with thick, murky Turkish coffee and tea leaves.

Turkish coffee is found in coffee specialty shops, or supermarkets with gourmet or specialty food leanings. The grounds are boiled in water and sugar. The result is a powerful, sweet, thick brew, poured into a coffee cup with a rounded bottom and a saucer. The querant must concentrate on his questions while drinking the coffee, and leave all the sediment and some of the liquid. Most of these syrupy remains are then poured into the saucer, while the rest is slowly swirled around the sides of the cup. The cup is then turned upside-down and set down, resting on the edge and middle of the saucer out of the syrup.

When the cup is turned right-side up, patterns will appear on the inside walls. In these patterns, certain images will begin to appear, sometimes vague and impressionistic, as in cloud formations. These images hold the key to the querant's question.

Sections of the cup represent different periods of time. The rim includes the present and near

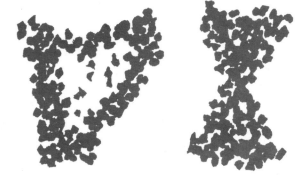

future; the bottom augurs the distant future. The handle represents the home or surroundings of the querant.

For reading tea leaves, the best results are obtained from China tea, or other tea with a minimum of tea dust. Tea should be brewed in a teapot without a strainer, obviously, so that leaves will be poured into the cup.

The seeker must drink the tea, leaving a little in the bottom of the cup. The reader takes the cup in his or her left hand, and slowly moves it around from left to right, three times. The leaves will be distributed around the sides and bottom of the cup.

INTERPRETATION OF THE ANCIENT SYMBOLS

Here are the meanings for commonly seen patterns and images:

Anchor Near the rim, abundant love; on the bottom, business success concerned with water or air; on the side, a commercial venture involving travel. If indistinct, misfortune in love.

Angel Good news.

Ants There will be many difficulties before success.

Apple Achievement.

Arrow Disagreement in a message or letter. With dots or dashes near, the disagreement concerns money.

Bat A fear of authority or an enemy.

Bell News, possibly of a wedding.

Bird Good luck, often a journey with good companions.

Branch Omen of a birth or new friendship.

Bridge Obstacles will be overcome.

Cage A proposal of marriage is imminent.

Cat This image signals a deceitful or treacherous friend.

Clouds Trouble; with dots or dashes, financial complications.

Clover Good fortune and happiness.

Comet Too much excitement, tension or unnecessary worry.

Cross Misfortune, sacrifice; on bottom of cup, a very serious problem; within a square, trouble can be averted.

Crown Highest honors and success through luck.

Daisy Desire for love and affection.

Deer Arguments should be avoided.

Dog A symbol of a true friend; if on the bottom, a friend is in need.

Duck Tenacity of purpose brings excellent results.

Eyeglasses Surprising events; caution is called for in business.

Fan A flirtation has already begun; a warning of an indiscretion.

Above: Ordinary tea cups will produce images and patterns that, when analyzed, will generate a portent for the querant. This reading will be a positive one because the shape of a bridge appearing in this cup predicts the surmounting of obstacles.

Flowers Honors, love; on the side of the cup, a new love or marriage is predicted; if on the bottom, an unhappy love affair is likely.

Grapes The querant is desirous of a love match.

Harp Romance, happiness.

Hourglass Decisions should not be rushed; if on the bottom, danger is forecast.

Key Enlightenment, new interests.

Kite Dangerous, risky times.

Ladder Advancement through personal ideas and ambitions.

Moon A full moon means romance; first quarter means new projects; last quarter indicates a need for caution.

Mountains Heavy travail must be finished.

Mushroom A mental or physical disturbance needs attention.

Pipe Open-mindedness is an asset.

Scissors If scissors appear near the rim, quarrels will end in separation; if near the handle, domestic unhappiness will occur; if on the bottom, reversals in job difficulties.

Snake An enemy or small misfortune.

Spade Industriousness is rewarded materially.

Square A protective agent is guarding against an accident or other dangers.

Star The symbol of destiny, the promise of the fulfillment of one's fondest hopes and aspirations.

Trees A promise of good health and comfort.

Wheelbarrow Alcohol could lead to social embarrassment.

The Path of Numerology

CRRRRD

Numerology is based on the belief that numbers, especially the primary numbers from one to nine, influence people's lives and personalities. Every person has numbers associated with his birth and name.

One of the oldest forms of occult lore, numerology dates back to the Babylonians and ancient Egyptians. Up through the Middle Ages, numbers were especially important to the Kabbalists. The Kabbala is the secret mystical lore of the Jews that is based on the *gematria*, the magico-philosophical science of numbers that revolves around the 22 letters of the Hebrew alphabet.

Numerology has attracted many followers in recent years, although the various systems used today differ somewhat from the ones used by the Ancients. Most of the present day systems are based on the theories of Pythagoras, the Greek mathematician and philosopher. Pythagoras believed that the universe was ordered mathematically, and therefore numbers were the key to the universe. In the past, numerology was considered strictly a form of divination, but today the adherents of numerology regard it as a method for analyzing personalities and potential as well.

The primary numbers from one to nine form the basis of all numerological systems. All numbers are then reduced to a primary number. The simplest and most popular system for reducing any number to a primary number is to add the figures of the number. If that number totals 10 or more, that number is reduced again. Thus, 25 becomes $2 + 5 = 7$, and 87 becomes $8 + 7 = 15$. Then 15 is reduced to 6. The same process is used to reduce dates. A number-letter equivalent is used to determine the number for names.

BIRTH NUMBERS

An individual's most important number is the birth number, which is found by adding up the numbers in one's date of birth. The month is assigned a numerical value, January being 1 and December 12. October, November and December—the tenth, eleventh and twelfth months—are reduced to primary numbers:

October (10) becomes $1 + 0 = 1$

November (11) becomes $1 + 1 = 2$

December (12) becomes $1 + 2 = 3$

If a person's date of birth is 28 January 1965, the equation is as follows: $2 + 8 + 1$ (for the first month) $+ 1 + 9 + 6 + 5 = 32$, which is reduced to $3 + 2 = 5$.

A person's birth number is obviously unchanging and therefore influences a person's character. The influence of the birth number, however, is tempered by various other numerological factors and should be viewed as a guiding factor rather than as a ruling force.

NAME NUMBERS

Every name has a number, obtained by translating the letters of the name into numbers as indicated in the chart below, and then adding their totals and reducing them to primary numbers.

1	2	3	4	5	6	7	8	9
A	B	C	D	E	F	G	H	I
J	K	L	M	N	O	P	Q	R
S	T	U	V	W	X	Y	Z	

From the letter J—the tenth letter—the letters are reduced to primary numbers. Thus, Z, the twenty-sixth letter, becomes $2 + 6 = 8$.

A person's name number is determined by the name usually used. Thus, Robert Persons, who goes by Bob, would use Bob rather than Robert.

B O B   P E R S O N S
$2 + 6 + 2 + 7 + 5 + 9 + 1 + 6 + 5 + 1 = 44 = 8$

A person's name number reveals acquired traits, and unlike the birth number can, of course, be changed. Numerologists believe that a change in

Previous page: The number eight, as seen here on a billiard ball, is the personal number of people who are materially successful, including the 'Material Girl' herself, Madonna. In the pool game named for it, however, the eight-ball can spell disaster if pocketed unintentionally.

the name, even just adding or dropping a middle initial, can influence one's life.

THE REVELATIONS OF THE NUMBERS

The **number 1** stands for the Sun. People with 1 as a birth number are strong-willed and driven. Ambitious and active, number 1 people are born leaders. With their dominant personalities, they are winners and innovators. These people are forceful and untiring and can achieve great things if their goals are well-directed. However, if misguided, people with 1 as a birth number can be self-centered, ruthless and tyrannical.

As a name number, 1 indicates vigor and a desire for action, but that action is best directed toward immediate goals rather than long-term ones. Determination is the hallmark of the name number 1. These people are successful, but they are apt to spend money freely once they have earned it.

The **number 2** represents a search for balance. People with 2 as their birth number have the ability to see both sides of a situation. This sense of fair play can work against them, as their desire for balance can cause them to waver indecisively. The sense of judgment that allows them to give good advice to their friends can prevent them from making up their own minds regarding their own affairs.

Those with 2 as their birth number should learn to deal with situations as they are rather than try to change them to suit their own desires. They should avoid situations that are marked by extremes or that call for decisions.

These people are gentle, kind and tactful. Number 2s are artistic, but as they are given more to thought than to action, they often lack the force they need to carry out their plans. Although they are charming and intuitive, 2s sometimes suffer from a lack of self-confidence. Their greatest fault is overgenerosity, and they should give the same consideration to themselves as they do to others.

As a name number, 2 denotes a person with a keen sense of judgment. But 2s are planners, not doers, and need associates to carry out their plans. In choosing their associates, 2s should rely on their sense of judgment rather than on emotion, as they may be wont to do.

The quest for balance can create an instability in people with 2 as their name number. Though generally happy, their emotional dispositions can make them restless and gloomy; 2s therefore should avoid situations that promote worry. They should make the most of their friendly natures and avoid arguments. These people get along well with their opposites—number 1s.

The **number 3** signals a talented individual. People with the birth number of three are quick learners. They are typically successful in their chosen fields as they are conscientious and independent. They excel at arts, sciences, sports—

anything that demands quick thinking and intuition.

People with this birth number like to be entertained. They attach a great deal of importance to pleasant surroundings and interesting people. Because they have a tendency to think only of the present, 3s should guard against neglecting their plans, thereby allowing others to profit from their ideas.

As a name number, 3 signifies competence and confidence. People with this name number can achieve great success, but 3s tend to be impatient and the promise of instant gratification may lure them away from a career path that offers more in the long run.

The **number 4** represents a steady and practical nature. People with 4 as their birth number have the ability to grasp new ideas quickly, but their temperament is such that they prefer to study a new idea completely.

Honesty, reliability, patience and perseverance are the characteristics of a person with 4 as their birth number. Professionally, 4s do well at any exacting task, such as research, or in scientific or technical fields.

As a name number, 4 stands for stability. Other people like 4s because they are dependable and trustworthy. Number 4s are even-tempered and good in an emergency. Though some may describe 4s as plodding, their endurance makes up for any lack of brilliance. Persons with 4 as their birth number should never underestimate themselves, for their traits will always be in demand.

The **number 5** indicates an adventurous, enthusiastic personality. Persons with 5 as a birth number enjoy traveling, feel at home anywhere, and are adept at learning foreign languages. Versatile and vivacious, 5s are open to new ideas and often act on impulse. They love the new and unusual and deplore routine. A drawback to their need for change is that 5s may overlook solid opportunities because they are always focused on what lies ahead rather than on the here and now.

As a name number, 5 signifies independence, both in thought and action. Persons with 5 as a name number prefer to learn through their own experiences rather than taking the advice of others. People of this type can be quite successful, providing they can control their restless natures. Ideally, those with 5 as a name number do best in situations where their flair for the dramatic and need for the unexpected are put to use.

The **number 6** represents sincerity. People with 6 as a birth number are dependable and honest. Other attributes include a cheerful disposition, a tolerant nature and an optimistic outlook. People of this sort are peacemakers, fostering harmony among their friends. They enjoy the finer things in life and do not hesitate to share with others.

As a name number, 6 betokens success, for this sort of person inspires confidence. Whether their goals are political or commercial, people with this name number attract followers and customers. They need not be radical in what they offer as long

as they provide what they have promised. 'Honesty is its own reward' is the creed of the 6. Their kind, caring personalities earn them many friends.

The **number 7** symbolizes knowledge. People with 7 as their birth number have scholarly, often poetic, natures and are often inclined to the fanciful. They are imaginative and intuitive and, oddly enough, analytical. Their preoccupation with things mysterious has a tendency to make them moody and depressed.

Number 7 people are inspired by solitude, and are drawn to artistic and philosophical endeavors. However, they become despondent if the rest of the world ignores them, which causes them to withdraw completely. To be happy, number 7 people need to overcome this tendency to withdraw and need to instead become more active.

As a name number, 7 holds the promise of great things. These people often become composers, musicians, philosophers or writers. To be successful in their chosen field, however, they must overcome their natural tendency to be dreamers, relying instead on careful planning. Financial independence or commercial success will be achieved only with the help of others, for practicality is not part of 7's character. People with 7 as a name number can become great leaders or teachers, as they understand others well and have the ability to inspire.

The **number 8** denotes material success. People with 8 as their birth number are effective planners, capable of carrying their plans to completion. Once their goals have been achieved, they go on to something bigger and better.

Number 8 people have strong, forceful personalities. They are demanding and expect—and get—perfection from their associates. Opposition does not deter them, and may, in fact, spur them on. These people often make great military or political leaders.

People with 8 as a birth number are driven by the need for wealth and power, and though they can be quite ruthless, those around them enjoy the benefits of number 8's success. Wealth and success are also the standards by which number 8 judges other people. The value of an object, too, is measured in terms of its monetary value.

As a name number, 8 seeks prosperity. These people have a constant need to be active and see things happening around them. Momentum is important, for if 8 slows down, progress will be hindered considerably. On occasion, however, a neglected or forgotten project can be turned into a profitable enterprise. Persons with this name number should avoid wasting time and energy. Their motto should be 'Think big and act big!'

The **number 9** is a powerful number, combining influence with intellect. Like 8, the number 9 promises success, but whereas number 8 people find their fortunes in the business world, 9s achieve success through more creative channels.

Persons with 9 as a birth number possess wonderful, magnetic personalities. If they are able to carry out their brilliant ideas in a practical manner, their success will know no bounds. They must understand their capabilities and desires, and set their goals accordingly.

As a name number, 9 betokens a person of influence. If they use their natural talents, these people are capable of accomplishing great things for mankind. Because they have the ability to influence people, 9s should be guided by high ideals. If they behave out of character, their strength is lost. People with 9 as a name number should avoid dull, boring situations, which tend to stifle their creativity.

THE SECONDARY NUMBERS

Some numerologists study the meaning of the numbers beyond the primary numbers of one to nine. There are various theories and beliefs about how these secondary numbers are interpreted. The most mystical of numerologists see significance in many numbers, while others hold that only the secondary numbers up to 22 (for the 22 letters in the Hebrew alphabet) are relevant. Most authorities, however, ascribe meaning to only a handful of secondary numbers: 11, 12, 13, 22 and 40. Of these, 11 and 22 are generally considered the most significant.

The **number 11** provides initiative that is lacking in two, the number to which it is reduced. The number 11 is strong enough to end the indecisiveness of two. As a name number, 11 contributes an assurance and boldness to the number 2's sense of judgment.

The **number 12** signifies completeness. It is the number of signs of the zodiac, the months, the tribes of Israel and the apostles, to name a few examples.

Below: In the Book of Revelation, the Bible points to 666 as the Mark of the Beast. Numbers have held great importance in many cultures and religions throughout time, and continue to do so in modern times.

Opposite page: Elvis Presley's Los Angeles hairdresser interested him in spiritual matters in the 1960s, including numerology, which Elvis used to determine a course of action. The key numbers in Elvis' life were 8 and 2001. Elvis was born 8/1/35. 8 + 1 + 3 + 5 = 17. 1 + 7 = 8. Elvis rented office suite 2001 in the Commerce Bank Building at 2001 Union Avenue. The overture to Elvis' Las Vegas shows was 'Theme from 2001: A Space Odyssey'. Adding up the date that Elvis died produces the number 2001: 16 + 8 + 1977 = 2001.

The **number 13** is typically identified with bad luck and the black arts, but in some instances it can be a positive force.

The **number 22** adds a dash of mysticism to the steady nature of the number 4 to which it is reduced. People of this sort tend to focus on the inner self, often to the point of ignoring the world around them.

As a name number, 22 straddles the line between eccentricity and genius. In some cases, 22 takes the exacting, mechanical skills found in the number 4 and develops them in new and unique ways.

Like 12, the **number 40** is another power number that denotes completeness.

NUMEROLOGICAL ANALYSIS

The first step is to consider the person's birth number, as this is indicative of the person's natural characteristics. The birth number is called the *number of personality.*

Next, the name number is analyzed. Called the *number of development*, the name number reveals developed traits. If a person's name remains unchanged, the power of the name number increases in terms of the person's career. If the person adopts a new name or takes a stage name, then a numerological analysis is based on this new number, the *number of attainment.*

A person's name also reveals additional information. A vowel vibration is arrived at by adding the numerical values of all the vowels in the name and then reducing the figure to a primary number. This figure is called the *number of underlying influence.*

When a number occurs frequently in a name that number enters into the analysis. This number is referred to as the *number of added influence.*

Some authorities contend that if the birth number is higher than the name number, a person is prone to adhere to the attributes described by birth number rather than those described by the name number. This may create internal conflicts as the individual struggles to develop the qualities of the name number. On the other hand, if the name number is the higher number, then those attributes will predominate, which means that natural characteristics of the individual are directed toward situations of his own choice. In other words, the person is likely to control situations rather than be governed by them.

An individual with the same birth and name number is apt to have a balanced, harmonious disposition. This type of individual is well-adjusted and able to take all things in stride, but it should be noted that few of the world's movers and shakers have such a balance.

The following examples of numerological analyses of well-known personalities illustrate the principles of this ancient lore.

The writer, director, comedian and jazz clarinetist **Woody Allen** is an excellent subject for analysis, because his vibratory numbers reveal many of the basic concepts of numerology.

Woody Allen was born on 1 December 1935, giving him a birth number of 4, as illustrated below:

$$1+1+2+1+9+3+5 = 22 = 4$$

In the case of Woody Allen, the higher vibration of 22 has clearly exerted its power, adding introspection, eccentricity and genius to the staid number four.

For his name number, Woody has both a number of development and a number of attainment. These numbers illustrate how a change in a name impacts a person's life and career. When he moved from his hometown of New York to Hollywood to write for television, he decided to rename himself 'Woody,' and to use his given name as the latter half of his stage name. Today, he is known the world over as Woody Allen:

W O O D Y   A L L E N
$$5+6+6+4+7 \ +1+3+3+5+5 = 45+4+5 = 9$$
$$6+6 \quad + \quad 1 \quad +5 = 18 = 1+8 = 9 \textbf{ (VOWELS)}$$

Woody Allen's number of attainment is the number 9, which signifies success and influence. While 8 is the number of material gain gotten through business, 9 signifies success through creative ventures, such as movie-making. There is a combination of influence and intellect inherent in the name number 9, and Woody Allen is definitely one of the most influential and intellectual of America's popular directors. The vowel vibration also works out to 9, strengthening the force of this already powerful number.

An analysis of Woody Allen's given name is equally illuminating:

A L L E N   K O N I G S B E R G
$$1+3+3+5+5 \ + \ 2+6+5+9+7+1+2+5+9+7$$
$$= 70 = 7+0 = 7$$

Seven is the name number which offers great promise, especially for writing, music and philosophy. Allen Konigsberg developed great skill at the first two avocations, and has extensively studied the third. The number 7 indicates a somewhat reclusive, intellectual nature, combined with an imaginative and analytical mind. Before Allen Konigsberg became Woody Allen, he spent much of his time alone, studying the artists (especially film makers) and philosophers whose names and ideas are employed throughout his movies.

Typically, people with 7 as a name number are depressed and obsessed with their thoughts, as is Allen's comic persona, who is based on Woody's previous incarnation as Allen Konigsberg. He struggled with his shyness, hoping to possess the courage to perform onstage. True to his number of development, Konigsberg was torn between soli-

Opposite page: Mae West's birth number of five gives her the enthusiastic nature which often led her to be the focus of scandals.

Right: Woody Allen's numerological analysis illustrates the tenet of how a name change may change a person's destiny.

tude, which offered security, and the attention and approval offered by an audience. Today, he struggles to preserve his privacy while being one of the most famous Americans living today.

Mae West was born on 17 August 1892, giving her a birth number of 5:

$$1+2+2+1+8+0+9 = 23 = 2+3 = 5$$

The birth number 5 explains West's enthusiastic nature. As a young girl, she was eager to learn, though she never had the opportunity to attend school. Instead, she got her education from performing, beginning in stock at the tender age of five. Several years later, with the itinerant ease of those of her birth number, she was travelling the burlesque circuit billed as 'the Baby Vamp.' By the age of 14, she was appearing on Broadway and in vaudeville, where she introduced the shimmy to the stage.

With the characteristic zeal of 5s, West tried a variety of endeavors throughout her life. At the age of 34, she wrote, produced and directed her controversial first play, 'Sex,' on Broadway. The show was considered scandalous, and West was jailed for 10 days on charges of obscenity. She directed, but did not appear in, her next play, 'Drag' (1927), which was a smash hit out of town—West was warned not to bring it to Broadway. With the daring and open-mindedness typical of 5s, her plays concerned controversial subjects handled in a bold manner. After three more stage successes, Paramount offered West a screen contract. In 1935, Mae West was the highest paid woman in the United States.

West's wide variety of talents is no surprise, considering the versatility of those with the birth number of 5. Her name number echoes her birth number of 5, intensifying her vitality and candor, as well as her flair for theatre and adventure.

M A E   W E S T
$$4+1+5 \; + \; 5+5+1+2 = 23 = 2+3 = 5$$

Exercising the independent thought innate to those with this birth number, West evaded the inevitable clash with the censors by co-writing her own scripts and couching her bawdy humor in *double entendres*. She continued to appear on stage and screen, with the exception of a 10-year retirement in the 1960s, until the age of 85.

Princess Diana was born Lady Diana Spenser on 1 July 1961, giving her a birth number of 7:

$$1+7+1+9+6+1 = 25 = 2+5 = 7$$

The number 7 indicates a natural ability as a teacher, which is certainly true in Princess Diana's case. Her brief career as a kindergarten teacher in London evidenced the easy rapport that she enjoys with children, including now, of course, her own sons, Prince Harry and Prince William.

Diana's vivacious personality is also reflected in her name number, 5.

L A D Y   D I A N A   S P E N S E R
$$3+1+4+7 \; + \; 4+9+1+5+1 \; + \; 1+7+5+5+1+5+9$$
$$= 68 = 6+8 = 14 = 1+4 = 5$$

Although the birth number of 7 predominates, the name number, or number of personality, is 5, which offers insights into Diana's independent and playful nature. Her mischievous hi-jinks with Sarah Ferguson, Duchess of York, were known to

Opposite page: Clint Eastwood *evinces the power of a vowel vibration to lend influence to an individual, allowing him to be a successful director and mayor, as well as an actor.*

Left: *Since her appearance in the public eye, Princess Diana— shown here with Prince William—has been called by three names, and the numerological configuration of each reveals her situation at the time that she was called by that particular name.*

have caused some little consternation at the palace.

Since Princess Diana is still known to much of the world simply as 'Lady Di,' an analysis of this nickname alone is warranted.

L A D Y   D I
$$5+1+4+7 \; + \; 4+9 = 30 = 3+0 = 3$$

Though Diana was immediately labeled 'Shy Di' by the press when they first discovered that she was Prince Charles' new love interest, they soon found out that her elusiveness was not due to a reticent personality. Rather, if an extraordinary situation is thrust upon a person with name number of 3, she will remain an observer until she can emerge with her usual confidence and competence, and still come out a blushing English rose.

After her marriage to Prince Charles, Diana received her number of attainment along with her new husband, new name and crown:

P R I N C E S S   D I A N A   W I N D S O R
$$7+9+9+5+3+5+1+1 \; + \; 4+9+1+5+1 \; + \; 5+9+5+4+1+6+9$$
$$= 99 = 9+9 = 18 = 9$$

The number 9 is the symbol of universal achievement, and indeed, Princess Diana is loved all over the world. Persons with 9 as a birth number are characterized by their powerful, magnetic personalities, and Diana is no exception. More than a decade after her marriage, Diana's fans are still devoted to the lovely future queen of England. They copy her hairstyles, hats and clothing, name their sons after her sons, their daughters after her and follow news about her in gossip magazines as well as in the news.

Clint Eastwood is one of America's greatest heroes: a strong, smart, defender of justice, a man of morals. In his personal life, he is an efficient and successful producer and director, former mayor of Carmel, California, and, of course, a movie star.

C L I N T   E A S T W O O D
$$3+3+9+5+2 \; + \; 5+1+1+2+5+6+6+4 = 52 = 7$$
$$9+ \qquad\qquad 5+1+ \qquad\qquad 6+6 \quad = 27 = 9$$

As a name number, 7 denotes Clint Eastwood's success as a film star. The characters he portrayed on screen represented the very essence of strength and confidence. Off screen, he projected an equally heroic, almost mythical, image. His image as a strong, competent man was partially responsible for his election as the mayor of Carmel, California.

Eastwood's ability to inspire others is attributable to his name number. He rose above a very difficult childhood, during which he and his family wandered restlessly all over the West Coast. Clint rarely spent more than a semester in any one school. After his astounding success as a film hero, Eastwood began directing, usually in movies in which he also starred. The vowel vibration 9 points to his ability to wield influence.

Shirley Maclaine was born 24 April 1934, making her birth number 9:

$$4+2+4+1+9+3+4=27=2+7=9$$

The birth number of 9 marked Shirley as one headed for great financial success through creative endeavour. Her dancing and acting talents have brought her great financial success, as have her books on topics such as reincarnation and out-of-body travel. Shirley's birth name was Shirley MacLean Beaty:

$$\begin{array}{c} \text{S H I R L E Y} \quad \text{B E A T Y} \\ 1+8+9+9+3+5+7 \; + \; 2+5+1+2+7 \\ =59=5+9=14=1+4=5 \end{array}$$

The number 5 reveals Shirley's inherently adventurous nature, and love of new ideas. With the love of travel typical for people with 5 as a number of personality, she maintains eight homes around the world. She spends her time travelling when not working or writing.

Her number of attainment comes from her stage name, which she adapted from her given and middle names:

$$\begin{array}{c} \text{S H I R L E Y} \quad \text{M A C L A I N E} \\ 1+8+9+9+3+5+7 \; + \; 4+1+3+3+1+9+5+5 \\ =73=10=1+0=1 \end{array}$$

Shirley Maclaine is indeed a number 1 personality: ambitious, active, and untiring. From the age of 16, she spent her summer vacations in New York, looking for dancing jobs. After high school graduation, she moved to New York and persistently tried to break into the world of Broadway, finally winning spots in the chorus lines of various Broadway shows. Her big break came in 1954, when the star of *The Pajama Game* broke her leg, and Maclaine, the understudy, went on. That night, she was offered a movie contract. Shirley went on to receive four Academy Award nominations in her career, winning the fourth for her performance in *Terms of Endearment*.

Not ready to rest on her laurels even after such success, Maclaine participated in politics and her own personal growth with all the vigor of the number 1 personality.

Winston Churchill was born on 30 November 1874, giving him a birth number of 7:

$$3+0+1+1+1+8+7+4=25=2+5=7$$

The birth number 7 hints at Churchill's artistic side. In the years between the First and Second World Wars, Churchill held several government positions, but he also filled his time with painting, lecturing and writing.

The 7, the most mystical number, also reveals Churchill's intuitive side. Several times in his lifetime, especially during the Second World War, Churchill exhibited great powers of intuition. On one occasion, the prime minister was entertaining at No 10 Downing Street. The guests were called to dinner just as a nightly air raid began. The air raids had become so much a part of daily life that no one considered interrupting the party—no one, that is, except Winston Churchill. Leaving his guests for a moment, he ordered his staff to bring all the food into the dining room and then to go down to the bomb shelter. Churchill then returned to his guests and continued with the meal. A few moments later a bomb hit the rear of the house, completely destroying the kitchen where the staff had been preparing the meal. Thanks to Churchill's premonition, he and his guests escaped unscathed.

Churchill's name number expresses the traits that made him a great leader.

```
W   I   N   S   T   O   N      C   H   U   R   C   H   I   L   L
5 + 9 + 5 + 1 + 2 + 6 + 5   +   3 + 8 + 3 + 9 + 3 + 8 + 9 + 3 + 3
            = 82 = 8 + 2 = 10 = 1
    9    +     6    +     3     +     9
            = 27 = 2 + 7 = 9 (VOWELS)
```

The number 1 symbolizes action and aggression, which is what Churchill brought to his role as Prime Minister during England's fight against Hitler in World War II. Courage, self-reliance and purpose are the hallmarks of number 1. The vowel vibration 9 strengthened Churchill's ability to guide the people of England. The frequency number 3, which occurs 5 times out of 16 numbers, points to Churchill's natural talent and versatility. Analysis of Churchill's name reaffirms many of the distinctive qualities he is noted for.

NUMEROLOGY IN DAILY LIFE

Numerology can play a part in an individual's daily life by explaining how a given day harmonizes with his birth and name numbers. The day is assigned a number, using the same method that is used to obtain a birth number. This number is then added to the individual's birth and name number and the total is reduced to a primary number. By following this formula, a person can determine which days are better suited for a specific activity.

For example, Perry Farrell wants to analyze the influence that 4 November 1992 ($4 + 1 + 1 + 1 + 9 + 9 + 2 = 27 = 2 + 7 = 9$) will have on his life. His name number is 1 and birth number is 2.

Birth number	= 2
Name number	= 1
Date number	= 9
Total	= 12 = 1 + 2 = 3

According to the summary below, this is a good day for Perry to attend successfully to numerous tasks.

*Opposite page: Shirley MacLaine's (**at top**) name number—five—reveals much about her, as does her number of attainment after she had chosen her stage name. Winston Churchill's (**below**) spiritual and intuitive sides are revealed in his birth number of seven.*

1   This is a day for action. Problems of a business, legal or practical nature can be solved on this day. However, as it represents a day of purposefulness, all plans must be kept simple and be carried out immediately. It is a day of opportunity.

2   This is a day of contrasts, one that fluctuates between the good and bad. It is a day for planning and weighing matters. If a decision is made, action is best delayed. The influence of 2 makes this a day fraught with indecision.

3   This is also a day of action. In contrast to a day influenced by the number 1, this day is suited to handling a variety of tasks. Much can be accomplished on this day. Troublesome tasks can be completed with ease and problems can be solved. It is a good day for business as well as pleasure.

4   This is a day suited for handling mundane and practical tasks. It is not a time for fun and relaxation, as people often find themselves preoccupied with nagging thoughts about the various chores they should be doing. This is not a day for important events or for gambling.

5   This is a day to expect the unexpected. It is a day of adventure, filled with vitality and the urge to travel and try new things. It is easy to get swept away with the moment, and one should exercise some caution so that the wild schemes dreamed up on this day don't backfire. If an idea has merit, however, this is the day to take risks.

6   This is a day of contentment and understanding. It is a day for communication with business associates, friends and family, as long as conflict is not involved. It is not a day to embark on new projects, to solve a problem, or to take on a challenge. This is a day to finish projects that have been carefully planned and thought out.

7   This is a spiritual day, well suited to reflection on the deeper things in life. It is a good day to study, conduct research, or work on artistic projects. This is also the time to contemplate, to consult with others and to finalize plans. The most mystical of days, strange things are likely to happen.

8   This is the day to think big. Smaller projects should be avoided unless they lead the way to something grander. Effort and action will bring results, and complicated issues can be settled on this day. It is the day to handle money matters—the bigger, the better—for this is the day that fortunes can be made.

9   This day holds the potential for accomplishing great things. It is the time to make important announcements, to make contacts, or to propose ideas. Long-held goals and personal triumphs of an artistic or competitive nature can be realized on this day. This is the day to win!

The Mystery of Dice Divination

*I*n the olden days, when someone hoped to escape their fate, they usually ran away, not to join the circus, but to follow the carnival instead. Many had committed horrible crimes, others were just leaving behind some sorrow, and some were just looking for adventure.

The carnies, as these people are known, live like Gypsies, moving from town to town, often doing whatever was necessary to coax a few pieces of silver out of the *gadjo*, the naive country people they bamboozled. One carnival named *Bella Fortuna* had an especially rough crowd of carnies. The first night they arrived in a town, they'd simply cheat at gambling, or do other small crimes at which they could not be caught. The second night, just before the company left town, they might sell one man's buggy to another, or send out a small gang to rob the houses of the people at the carnival.

A man named Pico was the most low-down and mean of all the carnies. He would have simply been a criminal instead of a carny, but he liked the admiration he got from the younger carnies for his

angry Gypsies. He leaned back. 'Sure, tell me how rich I will be.'

'No, we will decide upon the question. Is Pico in danger?' He rolled the dice.

By now Pico had realized that all the other carnies had deserted him. He held his breath, watching the dice spin out his fortune and then come to a stop.

'Ah, seven. You are a very lucky man, because although you seem to be in grave danger right now, the dice say that you are not now in danger.' He drew a gun from under his pancho and said, 'Unfortunately, these dice are loaded, and so they lie, as do you, Pico.'

And that was the end of Pico the carny.

Dice divination, like so many other forms of looking into the future, is a very ancient practice. The 'roll of the dice' has been performed for so many centuries that its roots are obscured, grown over by the passage of time.

Because the tools necessary for this form of fortune telling are rather small and light, dice divination has always been favored by itinerant people: travelers, Gypsies and others who want to keep their burdens light.

In this form of augury, the seeker chooses and ponders a question while an ordinary pair of dice is rolled, preferably from a glass or cup. The dice should be brand new, however, and they should then be set aside for divinatory purposes only. They should not be used for game playing and certainly not for gambling.

The seeker consults the list that corresponds to the numbers appearing on the dice. The number of the question then corresponds to the number of the answer. For example, the seeker chooses ques-

more devious deeds. He wasn't sure that he'd find as good an audience were he to go into the crime business for himself.

Some of the carnies had their 'lucky dice,' which were loaded dice they could sneak into craps games with the *gadjo*. When he put a certain spin on them, Pico's dice always came up seven.

One night, *Bella Fortuna* stopped out in the middle of nowhere to celebrate a particularly successful heist they had perpetrated. As they cackled and danced around an enormous bonfire, they did not see or hear the approach of the Gypsies.

When the Gypsies overheard talk of Pico and his latest robberies, they decided to meet these carnies and teach them a lesson. After all, these carnies were impinging upon Gypsy territory.

So the Gypsies entered the circle of carnival trucks, and approached the man who seemed to be the leader. They began to gamble on rolls of the dice. Pico sneaked out his loaded dice. When he had won all the money the Gypsies had, he started to put his dice away.

'Not so fast,' said one of the Gypsies, grabbing onto Pico's hand. 'Would you not like to know your future?'

Pico had been drinking whiskey and was not at all frightened, though he was surrounded by the

Previous page: *The roll of two-five presages an uneven romantic future.*

Above: *Death watches as a mortal takes his chances on the roll of the dice. The powers of any sort of divination should never be underestimated, even if the conduit to understanding is, to our minds, a game piece.*

Right: *Mercenaries throw dice in this woodcut by Anton von Woensam. Dice appear in almost every culture, eastern and western, throughout history.*

tion number two: Shall I be happy in love? The roll of the dice comes up as a two and a five. Answer number two on the list headed two and five is then consulted: 'Spasmodically.'

According to traditional rules governing this type of divination, only three questions should be asked by one person on a single occasion.

Instead of actual dice, a chart may be used of the 21 possible combinations, whereby the seeker chooses the combination with a pin-the-tail-on-the-donkey methodology: eyes closed, pointing to a square at random:

1-1	5-6	3-3
2-5	3-4	4-6

5-5	2-3	1-6	2-6	1-2
2-4	6-6	1-5	4-5	3-6
1-4	3-5	4-4	1-3	2-2

Selection of Inquiries

1 In what field does my future success lie?
2 Shall I be happy in love?
3 Am I in danger?
4 Where will I find the lost or missing article?
5 Will my proposed enterprise be successful?
6 Will my present wish be fulfilled?
7 What subject should now influence my thoughts?
8 Which person should I believe?
9 Should I change my occupation?
10 Does the one I love, love me?
11 Shall I become involved in legal affairs?
12 Are my opinions of a certain person accurate?
13 Shall I receive the money owed me?
14 What does the next year mean to me?
15 Shall I receive the present I want?
16 Shall I hear from my absent friend?

17 Shall I have many adventures?
18 Will my secret be discovered?
19 Shall I take my proposed journey?
20 Shall I achieve my ambition?
21 What does marriage hold in store for me?
22 How shall I know my future love?
23 How many romances shall I have?
24 What does the immediate future hold for me?
25 What maxim applies particularly to me?
26 When will the traveler return?
27 Where shall I find real happiness?
28 What period of the coming year should be most favorable to me?
29 Shall I ever achieve wealth?
30 Should I travel or remain at home?

Left: *A roll of the dice may indicate whether one will travel far and frequently, and when travel is advisable.*

Answers for the roll one-one

1 Steadfast adherence to your present occupation.
2 Yes, if you behave unselfishly.
3 Not if you act cautiously.
4 In a room or a closet.
5 If it does not depend on other people, yes.
6 It depends entirely on yourself.
7 Elevation, high position, progress, a leader.
8 The one who makes the most objections.
9 Only if you see a real opportunity.
10 If your love is sincere it will be reciprocated.
11 To your disadvantage, if you are not careful.
12 They are exaggerated.
13 Only if you press for it.
14 It will be a period of progress.
15 You may never receive it.
16 Not until you write to that person.
17 Not many, but a few important and exciting ones.
18 Probably not.
19 Yes.
20 You must work to achieve it.
21 Misunderstandings, but eventual happiness.
22 He or she will be the one most interested in your ambitions.
23 Three to five.
24 Unexpected news.
25 Discretion is the better part of valor.
26 When the moon is full.
27 In a foreign country.
28 The month of your birth.
29 Not while you long for riches.
30 Travel is advisable.

Answers for the roll one-two

1 Where you can act in an advisory capacity.
2 You should be.
3 No.
4 Somewhere in the house, perhaps in a closet.
5 Yes, if you have a capable associate.
6 It is too extravagant.
7 Travel, the future, absent persons, art.
8 One who flatters you the least.
9 It would be inadvisable at present.
10 Yes, if that one is certain of your love.
11 If you do, it will be as a minor witness.
12 No. They have been influenced by chance occurrences.
13 Not for a long time to come.
14 Happiness and enjoyment, but no great achievement.
15 You are expecting too much.
16 Yes, very unexpectedly.
17 Very few, if any.
18 Very probably. Too many know it already.
19 Not as soon as you expect.
20 You have too high an object of attainment.
21 Happiness, unless you deliberately destroy it.
22 One who is your opposite.
23 One too many.
24 Several enjoyable events.
25 Procrastination is the thief of time.
26 When he makes his fortune.
27 In your own home.
28 The month of June.
29 Only through an inheritance.
30 You will travel frequently, but not far.

Answers for the roll one-three

1 Steady work and constant attention to detail.
2 More than if you love not.
3 No, and not for a long time to come.
4 You may not have lost it. Look again.
5 You will not lose by it, but do not expect great gain.
6 After you have given up hope for it.
7 Home, family, affairs of the heart, a new project.
8 The one who believes you.
9 No, your present one should be satisfactory.
10 Your love will not be returned for many months.
11 You should avoid all court proceedings.
12 They have been influenced by false information.
13 Yes, during the next month.
14 Disappointment, but of a temporary nature.
15 Yes. The next big holiday.
16 When you are ready to resume your friendship.
17 No, because you instinctively avoid them.
18 Probably not. Few people wish to know it.
19 Exactly as you have planned.
20 After you have modified it, you may succeed.
21 A large family and many responsibilities.
22 One whose birth number corresponds to yours.
23 Very few.
24 An unpleasant surprise.
25 Such things take time.
26 When he is least expected.
27 In your future work.
28 All periods are about equal.
29 Only through long effort.
30 You will not profit by travel.

Answers for the roll one-four

1 Travel and new lines of work.
2 Temporarily.
3 Much less than you believe.
4 You may find it unexpectedly.
5 At first, but be prepared for unexpected loss.
6 Yes, but you may regret the fulfillment.
7 Marriage, harmony and understanding, new ventures.
8 The oldest and wisest.
9 You will have no choice in the matter.
10 Yes, at present; but you must strive to keep the love.
11 Too often.
12 They were a month ago, but they are not now.
13 Yes, through an unexpected meeting.
14 Unexpected changes and new scenes.
15 It is due you, but has been forgotten.
16 Yes, through an unexpected meeting.
17 Yes, under strange circumstances.
18 It will be learned while you are absent.
19 Sooner than you have planned.
20 No, but you will gain a new one.
21 Many surprises, disagreements, and reconciliations.
22 One whom you will meet in a distant place.
23 As many as a dozen.
24 A succession of surprises, some good, others bad.
25 A rolling stone gathers no moss.
26 When his mission has been fulfilled.
27 In pleasant company.
28 The late summer.
29 Probably, but you will not retain it.
30 You will find that much that you want is in foreign lands.

Answers for the roll one-five

1 Inventive or mechanical lines.
2 Partly, but never as much as you hope.
3 Slightly, but much less than you believe.
4 Through a friend or a servant; after a long search.
5 It should be; but you may demand too much.
6 Not if it depends upon someone else.
7 A building, water, a change, buried things, mystery.
8 One who comes to you secretly and unexpectedly.
9 Not if many people advise it.
10 You will probably never know.
11 Only through a quarrel with family or friends.
12 They are due largely to prejudice and imagination.
13 Yes, you will receive it in small payments.
14 Mysterious happenings and unexplainable events.
15 When the person you expect it from has been reminded.
16 In a peculiar way, through a mysterious message.
17 Not many, but surprising ones.
18 Not if you conceal all evidence of it.
19 A peculiar happening will detain you.
20 Only if you make it known.
21 Misunderstandings with your in-laws.
22 He or she will be an only child.
23 Few who really care for you.
24 A disagreement resulting in a necessary change.
25 All is not gold that glitters.
26 When he has spent all his money.
27 In study and research.
28 When most of the holidays come at the turn of the year.
29 Not unless you sacrifice love and ambition.
30 If you travel you may never return.

Answers for the roll of one-six

1 An active profession.
2 If you give more than you get, yes.
3 It has, but it is probably past.
4 You are almost certain to get it back.
5 Not if you begin it at once.
6 Only through the efforts of a stranger.
7 Trouble, dispute, lack of agreement, mistaken trust.
8 One who now doubts your sincerity.
9 Not unless someone demands your services.
10 That person doubts your love.
11 Yes, small but annoying ones.
12 They are utterly groundless.
13 Yes, only through an unexpected arrangement.
14 Temporary good fortune.
15 Never.
16 Not for a long time, as there is no reason.
17 Ones that seem important to you but are of little consequence.
18 You will foolishly reveal it.
19 Probably not.
20 Possibly, but it is not in your best interests.
21 Several years of happiness.
22 One whom you now dislike.
23 An average of two a year.
24 Delay and slight disappointment.
26 Pride goeth before a fall.
26 Within a fortnight.
27 In your dreams.
28 The rainiest week of the year.
29 Yes, if other persons fulfill their obligations.
30 Travel only if your friends advise it.

Answers for the roll two-two

1 Where courage is needed.
2 Yes, if your love is true.
3 It is always near, but never great.
4 In a hallway, a passage, or among documents.
5 Yes, if you begin at once.
6 Eventually.
7 A personal matter, illness, fear or anger.
8 The one whose reliability you have tested.
9 Not for at least three months.
10 Not now, possibly later.
11 Only to your own advantage.
12 They are true except for a few minor details.
13 Part of it, but do not expect the whole amount.
14 Increased income, but also increased expenditures.
15 Yes, when there is a full moon.
16 Not until your friend returns.
17 Some, when you least expect or desire them.
18 Not until it can be of little harm.
19 Yes, perhaps sooner than you may have planned.
20 Probably, but overwhelming desires may prevent it.
21 Trying times, but eventual happiness if you persevere.
22 One who is both wise and cheerful.
23 One that you will long remember.
24 A message that you have long awaited.
25 Perseverance is a virtue.
26 When he is no longer welcome.
27 In the 'great outdoors.'
28 Late autumn and early winter.
29 Not while you spend money as carelessly as you do.
30 Travel indicates much money for you.

Answer to the roll two-three

1 A partnership, or cooperative business enterprise.
2 More and more as time progresses.
3 To a slight extent, but it will not be serious.
4 On a shelf, stand, rack, or in a small room.
5 Not if it is of a hazardous nature.
6 Very soon, if it is practical and tangible.
7 A close relation, travel, similar things, news.
8 The one whom you have known the longest.
9 Not unless it offers immediate increase of income.
10 You can find out only by asking.
11 Not for the next two years.
12 They are true except for a few details.
13 Only after long and persistent demand.
14 A period of moderate progress.
15 When you next hear from or meet the giver.
16 As soon as he or she needs your help.
17 Not unless you seek them.
18 Not if you guard it.
19 Not unless a new reason for the trip presents itself.
20 Not unless you receive unexpected assistance.
21 Wealth, but doubtful happiness.
22 One whom you meet through an old friend.
23 Three or four of brief duration.
24 A slight obligation to an old friend.
25 Fine feathers do not make fine birds.
26 Just before a wedding.
27 In a place of quiet and solitude.
28 The third week after a severe disappointment.
29 Your opportunity is present, if you can grasp it.
30 Travel only to make a change of residence.

Answers to the roll two-four

1 An old and established business.
2 Not if you are content with things as they are.
3 Only if you deliberately ask for it.
4 On a shelf, a floor, or some flat place.
5 Not unless it is well established.
6 Its fulfillment is already under way.
7 Ancient or foreign things; distant scenes; philosophy.
8 One who is in accord with your present plans.
9 Vary your present one, if you wish, but do not change it.
10 Not if your likes and dislikes are opposite.
11 None of your own making.
12 They are true, but too critical.
13 Not unless you have a receipt for it.
14 Steady progress, but an unexpected loss.
15 It will follow a letter.
16 A message is already on the way.
17 No, you should try to avoid them.
18 It will be difficult to prevent it.
19 Exactly as you have planned it.
20 Only unexpected misfortune can prevent it.
21 A change in life; new interests, to which you will become adapted.
22 One whom you meet in times of trouble.
23 No more than you have or have had.
24 A period of quiet, with possible achievement.
25 Beauty is only skin deep.
26 When he had received a letter from home.
27 In a new business.
28 The second week after a holiday.
29 Probably not; but if you do, it will be great.
30 Travel only when absolutely necessary.

Answers for the roll of two-five

1 Peculiar and unusual occupations.
2 Spasmodically.
3 Very much, but from one source only.
4 Near water, or by means of a journey.
5 The chances are greatly against it.
6 Only after disappointment.
7 Property, real estate, source of income, money.
8 No one is particularly reliable.
9 To do so will mean either great success or disaster.
10 No, but another does.
11 If you do, you will regret it.
12 Not in regard to money or financial affairs.
13 In the next month or not at all.
14 A new interest, of doubtful value.
15 After you no longer need it.
16 A misunderstanding must first be mutually forgotten.
17 More than you desire.
18 Not if you caution a close friend not to reveal it.
19 No, because another will take its place.
20 No, not to the degree that you hope.
21 Either great happiness, or divorce.
22 One who will render you a great service.
23 That depends entirely upon yourself.
24 A doubtful acquaintanceship.
26 Time and tide wait for no man.
26 On a cloudy night.
27 In the midst of excitement.
28 The first week of spring.
29 Not while you work for other people.
30 Travel will bring you pleasure but not profit.

Answers for the roll of two-six

1 Work requires executive consultations.
2 Your attitude may be indifferent.
3 Not now.
4 Someone has found it. It will be recovered with dignity.
5 It needs someone with unusual enterprise.
6 Not while you count on it.
7 Speculation, gain, a child, a school, learning.
8 One who is the most doubtful.
9 Not if it means a change of residence.
10 The person concerned knows nothing about your love.
11 They may play an important role in your future life.
12 Not unless other people share them.
13 Yes, quite soon.
14 Small obligations and trifling annoyances.
15 At an appropriate time.
16 You will meet the friend at a social gathering.
17 Only if you travel with strangers.
18 By a child who may not reveal it.
19 Yes, with someone whom you do not expect.
20 Seven years from now, or not at all.
21 A new circle of friends.
22 One who is tall, athletic and versatile.
23 One in particular who will cause you much trouble.
24 An unexpected demand which must be met.
26 A roving bee gathers the honey.
26 He is now on his way and will arrive without delay.
27 In a garden of roses.
28 The first hundred days.
29 Not until you have saved a few thousand dollars.
30 Travel is advisable except by water.

Left: *To the question, 'Shall I ever achieve wealth?' a roll of three-five answers, 'Yes, if you locate the source.'*

Answers for the roll of three-three

1 Enterprise and leadership.
2 Only through marriage.
3 It lurks at every corner, but you can avoid it.
4 A child has it or knows about it.
5 It should be highly successful.
6 Beyond your expectations.
7 Loss, misfortune, retaliation, restitution, new plans.
8 The one who is willing to do what you wish.
9 Yes, if a real opportunity presents itself.
10 With a greater love than yours.
11 Those who seek to involve you will be disappointed.
12 You hold the person in too high esteem.
13 Yes, with interest.
14 A new and successful enterprise.
15 When you need it most.

16 Only through the efforts of another friend.
17 Not very many, but very fortunate ones.
18 Yes, but it will not matter.
19 Yes, and it will be longer than you have planned.
20 Yes, if you do not change your mind.
21 A golden wedding anniversary.
22 One who is nearly your own age.
23 No definite number, but two in particular.
24 The realization of a desire.
26 The early bird gets the worm.
26 On a summer afternoon.
27 Wherever you look for it.
28 The month after next.
29 No; but your closest friend will.
30 Travel especially in the summer.

Answers for the roll of three-four

1 Something requiring persuasion or salesmanship.
2 It is doubtful.
3 In an unexpected way.
4 It is probably safe, as no one has found or taken it.
5 No, but it will lead to a new and better venture.
6 Only if your own efforts can attain it.
7 Comfort, merriment, a pleasant place, companionship.
8 One who will soon make your acquaintance.
9 Not unless your present one is too problematical.
10 Very slightly.
11 Only through an accident.
12 They are wrong on an important point.
13 Not if it has been owed for more than a year.
14 Great but unappreciated effort.
15 You have no right to expect it.
16 As soon as that person can communicate with you.
17 Not unless you travel.
18 Not if you confide in those who wish to know it.
19 Very probably.
20 Only after much work.
21 The fulfillment of your desire.
22 When you lose interest in those you now admire.
23 Plenty.
24 A useless inspiration.
26 A bird in the hand is worth two in the bush.
26 When he receives a telegram.
27 In the memories of long ago.
28 The coming year is not very favorable.
29 Not unless you continually work overtime.
30 Travel now; it may be your last opportunity.

Answers to the roll of three-five

1 Literary or artistic pursuits.
2 Yes, if you are romantic.
3 Only when the moon is in the last quarter.
4 Recovery is doubtful, but search again.
5 It may mean financial loss.
6 It depends upon you.
7 A journey, distant messages, a friend.
8 One who is absent-minded.
9 Not without a more remunerative one available.
10 No. That person's love belongs to another.
11 Possibly, if you undertake new ventures.
12 Time alone can tell.
13 No, but you will receive its equivalent.
14 A renewal of old friendships.
15 On a day when the snow has fallen.
16 Not until the person returns.
17 Yes, during the next leap year.
18 Only through an unguarded message or letter.
19 Exactly as you have arranged.
20 Yes, by means of a journey.
21 A great adventure.
22 One who has the same interests as you have.
23 Two, principally: one tall, the other short.
24 Some new accessories.
26 Think twice before you speak.
26 On a holiday.
27 Through a hobby.
28 When the snow is on the ground.
29 Yes, if you locate the source.
30 Traveling is good for everybody.

Answers for the roll of three-six

1 Something involving space or mystery.
2 Not in your own community.
3 Sometimes, at night.
4 Chances of recovery are good, through a stranger or servant.
5 Yes, if it requires travel.
6 No, but another will.
7 Marriage, good fortune, partnership, agreement.
8 Your own opinions are best.
9 Not if it means a business connection with relatives.
10 No, but you can win the love you desire.
11 Not if you avoid undesirable strangers.
12 They have been influenced by false appearances.
13 After you have paid all you owed.
14 Comfort and enjoyment, but wasted opportunities.
15 After you have bought something like it.
16 Yes, but you will receive bad news.
17 Yes, if you make a long trip by air.
18 Yes, by one who cannot use it.
19 Yes, but you will alter your plans slightly.
20 It is doubtful.
21 Happiness and moderate wealth.
22 One who has many relatives.
23 Many at one time.
24 An unexpected trip.
25 A stitch in time saves nine.
26 On the first of the month.
27 In working for others.
28 The hunting season.
29 Not unless you already have it.
30 Neither will satisfy you.

Answers for the roll of four-four

1 Where personality and persuasive powers are needed.
2 Not during your first experience.
3 You are your only real enemy.
4 A relative may know about it. Search again.
5 Not unless it is well financed.
6 Not if it involves money.
7 Loss, misfortune, disaster, mourning, unhappiness.
8 Only one who offers you financial aid.
9 Decide after long consideration.
10 Yes, because of ignorance of your faults.
11 Yes, where money is concerned.
12 Yes, but they are not complete.
13 After you have forgotten it.
14 Misfortune which may be overcome later.
15 You will receive something entirely different.
16 Yes, when you have paid what you have owed the person.
17 Yes, in strange surroundings.
18 Yes, but you will not know it for a long time.
19 Lack of funds will prevent you.
20 Yes, but in a different locale.
21 More than you expect.
22 One who speaks a foreign language.
23 Three of different nationalities.
24 Something that will perplex and amuse you.
26 A fool and his money are soon parted.
26 Saturday night.
27 Where you think you have lost it.
28 When the leaves are falling.
29 You will not be satisfied with what you get.
30 Travel, if the direction is westward.

Answers to the roll of four-five

1 Matrimony.
2 If you do not expect too much.
3 Not at all.
4 On a shelf, in a cabinet, a drawer or a box.
5 Yes, but others will profit more than you.
6 Very soon, or not at all.
7 Discomfort, illness, a servant, a friend, a problem.
8 One who is distantly related to you.
9 Not unless you have money saved.
10 Yes, but it may not endure.
11 Only through your own desire.
12 Fairly well, but not exactly.
13 Only through legal action.
14 Difficulty in collecting money.
15 When you have renewed an old friendship.
16 Through the newspapers.
17 During one summer.
18 Yes, by someone who will profit from it.
19 Not until you have set your affairs in order.
20 No, but a friend will.
21 The realization of hidden virtues.
22 One whose age is five years different from your own.
23 None of consequence.
24 An idle rumor.
26 Don't cry over spilled milk.
26 At the time he has planned.
27 In collecting butterflies.
28 The football season.
29 You have one chance in a million.
30 You will have no opportunity to travel.

Answers to the roll of four-six

1 Affairs of state.
2 Not unless you change your ambition.
3 Not unless you interfere in other people's business.
4 It is in an automobile or in someone's house.
5 Not financially.
6 A letter may bring its realization.
7 A journey, gold or jewels, love, a brother, a message.
8 Your closest relation.
9 Only upon the advice of the one you know best.
10 Your love is reciprocated.
11 Only after marriage.
12 You should investigate further.
13 You will know within a few weeks.
14 A change in residence.
15 When you have made a journey.
16 Through another person.
17 Yes, but none may please you.
18 It will become known gradually and do no harm.
19 No, it will be unnecessary.
20 If you persist for many years.
21 Many worries, but much joy.
22 That person will be a childhood sweetheart.
23 Several.
24 An unexpected meeting.
26 Let well enough alone.
26 When he realizes his mistake.
27 You will always be looking for it.
28 The fifteenth of November until the fifteenth of December.
29 Possibly, through foreign investments.
30 If you travel, buy a return ticket.

Answers for the roll of five-five

1 In enterprises that require planning.
2 Yes, if you are willing to settle down.
3 From those who try to flatter you.
4 Not far away, beneath a tree or by a wall.
5 Yes, if you do not have many associates.
6 No, because it is unfair to others.
7 Confinement, imprisonment, a publication.
8 The one who offers nothing.
9 Not now. You will know when the time has come.
10 That person feigns love but may be insincere.
11 Possibly, through a false friend.
12 Regarding ability, yes; reliability, no.
13 You will be given a worthless check.
14 Realization of mistaken opinions.
15 Yes, but think well before you accept it.
16 Yes, but you had better avoid the meeting.
17 A few, but dangerous ones.
18 Not unless you tell a woman.
19 No, an unexpected visitor may change your plans.
20 It is within your reach, but enemies may prevent you.
21 Jealousy and a loss of friendship.
22 Through a letter.
23 More than your share.
24 Temporary good fortune that will not last.
26 Beware of the stranger bearing gifts.
26 When he remembers an appointment.
27 In a theater.
28 The first week of September.
29 Yes, if your present plans materialize.
30 Travel only under sunny skies.

Answers for the roll of five-six

1 In affairs of public benefit.
2 It will not be your fault if you are not.
3 Very seldom.
4 It is probably gone beyond recovery. It may be near water.
5 It is doubtful, as your plans are hardly practical.
6 Yes, when you work instead of wish.
7 Something worn or carried; a highway, means of communication.
8 One who is very impulsive.
9 You may make a foolish step if you do.
10 Not as much as you love.
11 Only if you procrastinate.
12 They are too impartial.
13 You should have had it long ago. Now you may never get it.
14 New friends and new interests.
15 When you cease to worry about it.
16 Yes, by long distance or special delivery.
17 Less and less every year.
18 It is really of little consequence.
19 Yes, but it may bring disappointment.
20 Probably not. You are apt to give it up soon.
21 Harmony, with quiet existence.
22 One who is practical and not excitable.
23 Very few.
24 Nothing unusual.
26 Variety is the spice of life.
26 A few days behind schedule.
27 When you make a schedule.
28 Early July.
29 Not unless you have extraordinary luck.
30 Stay at home while you have the opportunity.

Answers for the roll of six-six

1 Where conditions are harmonious.
2 Not if it restrains you from other interests.
3 Not at present.
4 It is probably in a box or a case of some sort.
5 It may prove to be too speculative.
6 Partly, but not enough to satisfy you.
7 Silver, something white, gain, possessions.
8 The one who is most influential.
9 It should prove greatly to your advantage.
10 Yes, but the person is too susceptible.
11 Possibly, as a material witness.
12 Yes, but you may foolishly change them.
13 Not soon, but it will be more than you expect.
14 Unexpected acquisitions.
15 Not soon, but it will be better than you expect.
16 Your friend has forgotten how to reach you.
17 Not if you search for them. They will come to you.
18 Yes, but surprising events will render it harmless.
19 A more desirable trip will probably take its place.
20 If you really want it, yes.
21 True happiness, but many sorrows.
22 Your first meeting will be at night.
23 A sufficiency.
24 A stroke of wonderful fortune.
26 It's a long lane that has no turning.
26 After many difficulties have been surmounted.
27 Through lasting friendships.
28 Springtime.
29 Yes, but it will be of little use to you.
30 When you travel, go to familiar places.

How Dreams Shape Our Destiny

⊕⊕⊕⊕⊕

'We are such stuff as dreams are made of,' wrote William Shakespeare almost 400 years ago. But what are dreams made of? Since the dawn of recorded time, man has been fascinated by dreams and what they signify. An ancient Egyptian papyrus dating back to 1350 BC contained explanations of the good and bad signs found in dreams. According to the Egyptians, a dream about losing one's teeth, for example, was an omen that the dreamer's relatives were plotting his death.

About 150 AD, Artemidorus, an oracle, offered his version of a 'dream dictionary,' a guide to interpreting and analyzing dreams. Artemidorus divided dreams into two categories: those that dealt with everyday life and those that foretold the future. His interpretations were passed down to succeeding generations for the next 1000 years.

The interpretation of dreams gained credence once again in the nineteenth century with the theories of Sigmund Freud. Freud argued that dreams hold the key to our subconscious sexual desires that

THE EIGHT TYPES OF DREAMS

Today, popular theory holds that dreams can be classified into seven archetypal categories. Some authorities, however, add an eighth type.

Dreams of affluence: In a dream of this sort, the dreamer acquires a prize of some sort. This could take the form of becoming a business tycoon or winning the lottery. In some cases, the dream involves fame rather than fortune.

Dreams of frustration: In this type of dream, the dreamer is never able to accomplish a seemingly simple goal, such as trying to pack a trunk or suitcase or locate a parked car. In other examples, the dreamer may need money but have no way of obtaining it, or may be trying to catch a plane or a train.

Dreams of travel: Dreams of this sort can be concrete, as in going someplace, or abstract, as in simply flying through the air or drifting through space. They generally indicate a need for freedom or the desire to possess something.

Dreams of falling: The dreamer is falling from a skyscraper, a bridge, an airplane or other high place. Simply the sensation of falling is a common dream experience. People typically wake up, usually with a start, before they land. The old wives' tale goes that the dreamer will die if he or she fails to wake. These dreams often represent a situation the dreamer has been worrying about.

Dreams of being chased: The dreamer is pursued by another person, an animal or the forces of nature, such as a flood or an avalanche. The menacing force is symbolic of a hidden fear.

Dreams of being trapped: In these dreams, the dreamer is in a cellar, cave or prison and unable to escape. A similar type of dream involves a dangerous situation in which the dreamer is likely to experience physical harm, such as an explosion or the collapse of a building. These dreams are interpreted as a hidden fear.

Dreams of being naked: Dreams of this sort are often an indication that the dreamer is going through a period of frustration or is suffering from feelings of inadequacy. Dreams involving forgotten appointments or other examples of personal negligence, such as failing an exam, can be interpreted in a similar manner.

Dreams of violence: The dreamer is responsible for physically harming another individual. In extreme cases, the dreamer kills someone else. Such dreams are indicative of suppressed anger on the part of the dreamer.

have been suppressed since childhood. Through psychoanalysis, patients come to understand the meaning of their dreams and thus resolve emotional issues.

Carl G Jung, the noted Swiss psychiatrist, differed with Freud on various points. While Jung too believed that dreams offered a wealth of information once analyzed, he questioned Freud's emphasis on sexuality, which Jung believed was only one theme that might emerge from dream analysis. Jung proposed that the images in dreams were symbols that belonged to what he termed the collective unconscious. In his work, Jung had noticed that certain symbols and images, such as the wise old man or the evil serpent, appeared in many people's dreams. Moreover, these symbols transcended cultural barriers. In short, there seemed to be common symbolism even though there did not appear to be any sort of common denominator—apart from the human psyche. This is not to say that a dream about a horse, for example, will always have sexual connotations, for no individual symbolic image can be said to have a dogmatically fixed, generalized meaning.

Previous page: A mask is symbolic of a deception. If the dreamer encounters a person wearing a mask, that individual is hiding something from the dreamer. If the dreamer is wearing the mask, then he is the one hiding the truth.

Above: Dreams of affluence and fortune are one of the eight archetypal dreams recognized by dream analysts.

Opposite page: By analyzing one's dreams of being chased (*at top*), the dreamer may discover and come to terms with unacknowledged fears, or, if the dream involves committing violent acts (*below*), unacknowledged hostilities.

For both Jung and Freud, dreams were triggered by the individual's internal struggles and desires, and if analyzed could provide therapeutic value. Neither, however, completely discounted the possibility that dreams may be caused by forces outside the dreamer's own mind, such as another individual sending a message to the dreamer telepathically. Freud rejected the notion of precognitive dreams—dreams that foretold the future—but he was willing to concede that telepathic dreams were a possibility, concluding that sleep might be a state that would permit the transference of thought between people.

Even as Freud was formulating his thesis, several prominent British scientists were studying the possibility of telepathic dreams at the Society for Psychical Research (SPR). Founded in 1882, the SPR was created to research all kinds of paranormal events, including telepathy, clairvoyance and spiritualism. The SPR's dream research disclosed 149 dreams in which the dreamer seemed to have received a message from an outside source. Of added interest to the researchers was the fact that a majority of the dreams dealt with the death of someone known to the dreamer. To further investigate this phenomenon, the SPR researchers sent out over 5000 questionnaires asking people if they had dreamed of the death of someone they knew in

Above: *Carl Jung discovered that certain symbols and images, such as the evil serpent, appeared in many people's dreams. Moreover, he noted that these symbols transcended cultural boundaries.*

Opposite page, top: *The appearance of an angel in a dream portends good news or protection from evil.*

Opposite page, bottom: *Dreams of being naked are often an indication that the dreamer is going through a period of frustration or is suffering from feelings of inadequacy.*

the last few years. The results convinced the SPR that something more than chance was at work.

But what was that something else? Throughout the ages, people have had dreams that foretold the future, oftentimes of tragedy and death. Samuel Clemens, better known to the world as Mark Twain, foresaw the death of his brother, Henry, in a dream. The year was 1858 and Sam Clemens was an apprentice pilot on a Mississippi River steamboat, the *Pennsylvania*. Henry worked as a clerk aboard the same boat. One night in a dream Sam saw the body of his brother laid out in a metal coffin resting on two chairs. On his chest lay a bouquet of white flowers with a single red flower in the center.

The *Pennsylvania* continued on its way down the Mississippi and the two brothers parted company when Sam joined the crew of the *Lacey*. A few days later, Sam heard the news that the *Pennsylvania* had blown up near Memphis. There, he found Henry, dying from the burns he had sustained in the accident.

Though Henry was a stranger to the people of Memphis, several women of the city had collected money to purchase a coffin for him, a metal one rather than the typical pine. When Sam went to pay his final respects to his brother, he found Henry laid out just as he had seen him in his dream—except for the flowers. And then an elderly woman entered the room and placed a bouquet like the one Sam had seen in his dream on Henry's chest.

In a dream, Abraham Lincoln heard the sounds of people crying in grief. He followed the sound of the mourners to the East Room of the White House, where he saw a body lying in state. When he asked the mourners who died, the eerie reply came: 'The President. He was killed by an assassin.' Not long afterward, the President's dream became a horrible reality.

JW Dunne, a British aviator and aeronautical engineer, experienced several dreams that he believed were prophetic. During the Boer War in South Africa, Dunne dreamed of a volcano about to erupt. He saw himself on a neighboring island, pleading with French officials to send ships to rescue the 4000 people stranded on the island. Soon afterward, Dunne saw a newspaper account in the *Daily Telegraph* of a volcanic eruption on the French-governed isle of Martinique. The report was eerily reminiscent of Dunne's dream: The survivors were removed by ship, and the number of victims reached 40,000—Dunne's dream was off by a tragic zero.

In another dream, Dunne encountered three men in Khartoum, in the Sudan. They told him they had just come all the way from the southern tip of Africa. The next morning, Dunne read in the morning paper that the 'Cape to Cairo' expedition had just arrived in Khartoum. Prior to that morning, Dunne had never heard of the expedition. On another occasion, Dunne dreamed of a train plummeting off an embankment near the Forth Bridge in Scotland. Several months later Dunne's dream became reality as the *Flying Scotsman* crashed not 15 miles from the Forth Bridge.

Dunne was a well-educated man, not the sort to invent the stories, but some people wondered if he hadn't simply imagined the dreams after reading about them. Others suggested that perhaps his dreams were the product of mental telepathy with the reporters on the *Daily Telegraph*. Dunne concluded that some dreams are simply prophetic.

Scientists continued to be intrigued by the possibility of dream telepathy, and in the 1940s Wilfred Daim, a Viennese psychologist, conducted the first series of dream telepathy experiments. Unfortunately, Daim's research encountered a major stumbling block. Even if the dreamer had received a telepathic message, it was virtually impossible to pinpoint the precise moment the dreamer had received the message. To complicate matters further, upon awaking the dreamers often had only vague memories of their dreams, rendering them useless from a scientific perspective.

It wasn't until 1953, when Dr Nathaniel Kleitman discovered REM sleep, that researchers could come closer to understanding the nature of dreams. Kleitman and his team of researchers at the University of Chicago determined that sleep consists of two separate phases. In the first phase, physical and mental activity subsides, but in the second phase the sleeper's breathing is irregular,

his brain activity is similar to a waking state, and his eyes move rapidly under closed lids. When sleepers were awakened during the first stage, they generally did not recall dreaming. In the second stage, dubbed REM for rapid eye movement, sleepers reported that they were dreaming. Researchers discovered that these REM phases occur about every 90 minutes, lasting roughly an hour. Additional research suggested that REM sleep is essential for sleepers, for when they are deprived of REM sleep the tendency is to dream more the following night.

Kleitman's research provided a major breakthrough in the study of dreams. Researchers could now determine when a subject was dreaming and could thus wake him up to question him about his dream. When awakened in the midst of a dream, the subjects could vividly recall their dreams.

DREAM SYMBOLS AND IMAGES

Accordion Dreams featuring accordions are less common today than they were in the past. Hearing an accordion is interpreted as a sign that the dreamer is disappointed. An out of tune accordion represents an unhappy state of mind. Playing an accordion betokens marital bliss.

Acrobat An acrobat is an omen of a dangerous scheme. If the acrobat falls, the scheme should be avoided. A person dreaming that he is an acrobat is expressing a need for appreciation.

Actor, actress Dreaming about an actor or actress represents a desire for fame and recognition.

Airplane A plane taking off can be interpreted as a sign of high hopes for the future. However, if the plane is still on the ground, the dreamer seeks to avoid a troublesome situation.

Anchor An anchor indicates a need for permanence in one's personal or professional life. An anchor tied to a ship symbolizes the desire to break free from an unpleasant situation.

Angel An angel is the symbol of glad tidings, representing good news or protection from evil.

Animals A wild animal or one that is out of control represents a desire for sex. However, a pet signifies contentment and companionship.

Ants Ants represent minor irritants.

Apples Dating back to the legend of Adam and Eve, apples are said to represent sex. Ripe apples denote good luck, while fallen apples signify failed plans.

Automobiles Dreaming of an automobile represents the desire for financial gain, while a moving car is traditionally interpreted as sexual desire. A car accident is said to be a warning of a complication in one's life.

Ax An ax is the symbol of happiness after a struggle. A sharp ax is an assurance of financial success, while a dull one represents a downturn of

Opposite page, top: To dream of an automobile indicates a desire for financial profit.

Opposite page, bottom: A baby may symbolize many different things. A happy baby signifies friendship, while a sleeping baby indicates the desire for a mate.

Above: A symbol such as a wild animal may represent the dreamer himself, or a person or situation with which the dreamer is involved.

economic conditions. A broken ax stands for a disappointment.

Baby A baby has various meanings. A crying baby represents disappointment, while a happy baby signifies friendship. A sleeping baby is frequently interpreted as the desire for a mate.

Ballet A ballet signifies infidelity and jealousy.

Banana According to ancient lore, a banana represents a minor illness. An overripe banana indicates boredom, either with work or a partner.

Bath, bathing Taking a bath, especially more than one, denotes an interest in the opposite sex. For the person who has previously been married, a bath is a sign of remarriage. Some interpretations suggest feelings of guilt, while others indicate a physical problem.

Bats Bats signify bad news and sadness.

Bear Bears are said to foretell a situation in which the odds are against the dreamer. A bear can also represent a rival, either personally or professionally.

Bells The tolling of bells augurs the death of a friend or a loved one.

Bicycle Riding a bike uphill betokens good news, while riding a bike downhill forewarns of misfortune.

Birds A dream of a bird perched in a tree signifies unexpected happiness, a flying bird symbolizes prosperity, a wounded bird denotes depression caused by a family member, and talking birds are a warning of gossip.

Blindness Dreaming of a blind person indicates a person in distress. If the dreamer is the blind person, that is a sign that he is not seeing his own faults.

Blindfold A blindfold signifies a temporary setback.

Bomb A bomb represents a situation that will be a source of great distress for the dreamer.

Books Books indicate intellectual pursuits. Shelves of books signify the need for more discipline where work is concerned, while empty shelves point to losses caused by a lack of knowledge.

*Disappointment may be represented in dream by different symbols, including a bridge (**above**) or a church (**opposite page, top left**).*

*Opposite page, top right and **bottom**: A clock or a white cat may symbolize the death of a friend.*

Bridge A dream of crossing a bridge signifies overcoming an obstacle, while passing under a bridge denotes a burdensome problem that will take some thought to solve. A long bridge that seems to vanish in the distance indicates a loss or a disappointment in love.

Canoe Paddling a canoe in still waters is interpreted as being able to run a business successfully. However, a canoe in rough waters is the sign of discontent, either personally or professionally.

Cat Legend holds that a cat is symbolic of a woman. An angry cat denotes a female enemy, while a thin cat signifies bad news about a friend. A white cat is a sign of a youthful indiscretion. A white cat has also been interpreted as a loss for an adult.

Cemetery A dream about a cemetery represents news from someone from the past. To the person who has lost a spouse, a cemetery betokens a remarriage or other major life change.

Cherries Cherries are a traditional symbol of good luck.

Children A dream of children playing and laughing is a sign of happiness. Conversely, unhappy children represent a disappointment. A sick child betokens monetary problems.

Church A dream of a church represents a wish come true. However, if the church is in the distance, it represents a disappointment. Entering a church is said to signify marriage. According to some authorities, a church symbolizes the nurturing, protective characteristics of women.

Clock A clock or watch indicates that the dreamer is obsessed with time. A striking clock portends the death of a friend or loved one, or even oneself.

Clouds Dark clouds warn of dark times ahead.

Dancing According to traditional interpretations, dancing indicates happiness. Modern analysts, however, see dancing as a sign of sexual desire.

Dogs Friendly dogs denote friendships, while angry, biting dogs signify anxiety. Freudian interpretations hold that mad dogs represent sexual desires. According to ancient dream lore, a white dog signified marriage for a woman and business sense for a man, a baying dog symbolized a death in the family, and a growling dog indicated depression.

Driving Driving a car in a dream expresses a desire for independence, while speeding signifies a need to escape. If the dreamer is the passenger, he has faith in the driver.

Drowning Popular theory interprets a dream about drowning as the desire to be reborn.

Elephants Elephants are symbols of power, force and memory.

Fire Dreams of fire represent sexual desires. Traditional interpretations regard fires as good luck: A fire at home indicates a happy home life, while a fire at one's place of business signifies prosperity.

Gate A dream of a closed gate warns of problems to come, while a broken gate is a failed

These pages: A white horse signals prosperity, while a horse of a different color does not bring such glad tidings. According to some dream analysts, both guns and goats are symbolic of virility, while a nun signifies a need for contemplation or a change in a woman's circumstances. For people who attended parochial school, a nun may represent authority or discipline.

endeavor. Swinging on a gate indicates a light-hearted nature.

Goat   A goat symbolizes virility.

Grass   Dreams of grass are thought to be prophetic. A vast expanse of grass augurs the fulfillment of one's goals, but if the dreamer should crush the grass, the completion of one's goals will be fraught with problems.

Gun   The sound of a gunshot is interpreted as a warning. Shooting a person signifies dishonor. According to Freudian analysis, a gun, like a knife or dagger, symbolizes male sexuality and desires.

Hat   A hat signifies a change of place. Losing a hat is seen as a bad omen.

Horse   A white horse means prosperity, a black horse, deception. A runaway horse warns of financial difficulties. According to modern interpretations, horses are symbols of sexual passion.

House   Building a house signifies a major life change. Dreaming of an elegant house indicates the desire to improve one's social status. A house that is falling apart is a sign that finances need to be attended to. An unpleasant house may be indicative of discontent at home.

Island   An island is a symbol of happiness and comfort. However, if the dreamer is seeking refuge on the island, it represents a desire to escape. If the island is populated with many people, the dreamer desires friends.

Jewelry   Fine jewels denote high ambitions, while broken jewelry signifies disappointments, and tarnished jewelry, business problems. A gift of jewelry is said to represent a happy married life.

Key   Dreaming about a key indicates a change ahead. A key that is broken symbolizes grief, while lost keys signify an unpleasant situation. Finding a key is a good omen.

King   A king signifies authority. Dreaming of being king indicates a desire to control others, while seeing a king shows a need for direction.

Lamb   A lamb frolicking in a pasture is a sign of happiness, while a lost lamb signifies uncertainty. A dead lamb is a bad omen.

Lightning   A dream of lightning represents love.

Lock   A lock represents confusion. If the lock is on a door or a trunk, the dreamer desires to see what lies beyond the lock, but in order to understand the dream, it is necessary to analyze the meaning of the door or the trunk.

Mice   Dreams of mice represent deception and insincerity. Ancient dream lore holds that a young girl dreaming about mice should be forewarned of a scandal. Modern interpretations regard mice as sexual symbols.

Mountains   Mountains are symbolic of the desire to attain great heights. If the dreamer reaches the top of the mountain, his goal will be fulfilled. Hazards encountered along the way signify life's frustrations.

Music   Hearing music is a sign of good luck. If the dreamer is disturbed by the music, the music portends emotional uncertainty.

Needle   Dreaming of threading a needle signifies problems that can be solved only through

patience. Breaking a needle represents the urge to be alone, and sewing with a needle indicates a friend in need.

Newspaper   Reading a newspaper is a warning that one's reputation is in danger. If the dreamer is trying to read but cannot see the words, business difficulties will follow.

Nuns   Dreaming of nuns indicates a need for spiritual reflection. If a woman dreams that she is a nun, she is discontented with her situation in life.

Nurse   Nurses signify good health, but to dream that one is a nurse signifies a need to have friends.

Oak   An oak tree filled with acorns signifies a promotion and a raise, while a forest of oak trees betokens prosperity.

Ocean   A calm ocean is a sign of good fortune, while a rough ocean signifies danger. Various other interpretations view the ocean as a sign of death, a desire to be reborn or the opportunity to start again.

Oranges   According to traditional interpretations, an orange is a sign of lost love for a woman

and unexpected business complications for a man.

Owl The owl is commonly regarded as a sign of wisdom. Other interpretations see the owl as representing gossip. The hoot of an owl signifies ill health or bad news about a friend.

Paralysis Dreams of paralysis are fairly common. In these dreams, the dreamer cannot move, walk, talk or scream. The paralysis signifies a difficult problem that the dreamer cannot solve during his waking hours.

Peaches Dreaming of eating peaches symbolizes unattained wealth or unrequited love. Peaches on a tree mean that hard work will be rewarded.

Pearls A gift of pearls symbolizes a celebration. Breaking a strand of pearls or losing pearls represents misfortune.

Pears Pears betoken surprises and good health, followed by disappointments and temporary illness.

Pebbles Pebbles in dreams stand for petty jealousies.

Pregnancy Dreaming of pregnancy represents anxiety and impatience.

Pyramids Pyramids symbolize the desire for new surroundings or new areas of interest.

Railroad A railroad with winding tracks represents the changes and complications that exist throughout life.

Rain Dreams of rain are prophetic. Watching rain from indoors augurs prosperity, while being in the rain warns of a slowing of plans. A rainstorm is a sign of mental turmoil.

Reptiles Reptiles of all kinds represent obstacles. One snake denotes an argument, and two stand for two friends that will deceive the dreamer. The snake also symbolizes male sexuality.

Ring A ring is a symbol of friendship, love and marriage. Receiving a ring foretells of meeting a new friend, while a broken ring denotes a separation from a loved one.

Shoes Old, worn shoes have traditionally been interpreted as a message to the dreamer to be tolerant and respectful of others. Untied shoes warn of misfortune, while having shoes shined is a sign of important changes ahead.

Smoke Dreaming about smoke indicates a confused state of mind.

Snakes See Reptiles.

Snow A snowfall warns of a crisis that may be costly as well as emotionally distressing. A snowstorm represents frustration. Climbing a snow-covered mountain indicates a business disappointment.

Spider A spider symbolizes a worrisome situation. This sort of dream is apt to recur until the dreamer has solved the situation.

Sports Dreams about baseball, football, soccer and other sports represent a need for harmony and teamwork. People who dream about sports generally expect others to act fairly.

Stair According to some psychoanalysts, dreams about stairs reveal sexual desires. Traditional interpretations regard these dreams as

Opposite page, top: A sunset is a beautiful sight during waking hours, but when seen in a dream it can presage economic troubles.

Opposite page, bottom: A dream of a football game indicates a desire for harmony and teamwork.

At right, top and bottom: Most people probably see snakes and owls more often in dreams than in real life. The snake may represent—among the many interpretations of this recurrent symbol—duplicity and betrayal, or male sexuality. As in folk tales, the owl is associated with wisdom, but also with gossip, heresy, ill-health and bad omens concerning a friend.

signs of good fortune. However, walking down the stairs signifies bad luck in business and love, while falling down the stairs means that enemies will create obstacles.

Sun A sunrise is an omen of happy times, while a sunset warns the dreamer to be cautious where money and property are concerned. The sun showing through the clouds predicts prosperity.

Swan A white swan foretells of happiness and prosperity, while a black swan is a warning to avoid immoral situations.

Swimming When the dreamer is enjoying the sensation of swimming, the dream indicates the desire to have fun and enjoy life. However, if swimming is a struggle, the dreamer is going through a distressing period. Swimming with others indicates a desire to make new friends.

Thief A thief in a dream means that someone has usurped the dreamer's rights. However, if the dreamer is the thief, he has has usurped the rights of another.

Tomato Dreaming of a tomato indicates a desire to socialize. Ripe tomatoes are symbolic of a happy marriage.

Torture Dreaming about torture reveals a conflict concerning love or money.

Trees Trees are symbolic of pleasure and success. Dead trees, however, portend losses. Cutting down a tree is a sign to avoid quarrels.

Trunk Dreaming of packing, opening or closing a trunk or suitcase reveals a desire for change. A trunk that is never packed or closed symbolizes a frustrating situation.

Tunnels Tunnels are symbolic of insecurity. Being trapped in a tunnel reveals a desire to escape. Some psychoanalysts interpret tunnels as a symbol of sexual interests.

Umbrella Dreaming about umbrellas reveals personal misunderstandings.

Violin A violin represents esteem, and possibly awards. A broken violin betokens separation from a loved one.

Volcano Volcanoes symbolize emotions and act as a warning to those who are quick to lose their temper.

Walking Walking at night, or on a rough or winding path indicates a distressing situation.

Walls Walls are symbols of frustration or the inability to attain a goal. Breaking through a wall in a dream signifies overcoming obstacles to reach one's goal.

War Dreaming of war during times of peace symbolizes family problems.

Watch Watches are signs of prosperity.

Water Clear water is a sign of wealth and happiness, while muddy water signifies illness. Playing in water indicates a desire to be loved, and rough

*Opposite page: A volcano (**top**) is a fairly obvious image, foretelling an eruption of emotion instead of lava. Many symbols can be revealed by referring to old fairy tales, such as the wolf (**bottom, left**) representing something or someone who is dangerous and disguised as harmless.*

*Some dream images may actually appear as hidden puns in dreams, such as this image of a train entering a tunnel (**bottom, right**), signifying the light at the end of the tunnel.*

Above: Dream imagery is often an exaggeration of a real situation. Thus, a dream of war may mean personal wars—arguments with friends and family.

water symbolizes difficult times leading to success. Jumping into water represents a desire for a second chance.

Window A closed window is a sign of frustration, while a broken window signifies a broken heart. Crawling through a window reveals bad intent.

Wolf Like the old adage about a wolf in sheep's clothing, a dream about a wolf signifies a friend who is really an enemy.

Yacht Dreaming of a yacht reveals a desire to be free.

Zoo A dream about a zoo denotes a feeling of being trapped or of helplessness.

Often the best way to interpret your dreams is to ask yourself what a particular image means to you personally. A woman was suffering from recurring nightmares about sharks. She hoped to end the nightmares by understanding the underlying fears that were causing them, so she embarked upon a study of dream interpretation. She learned that Freud saw sharks as threatening images of female sexuality, but the woman couldn't make a connection with that fear. Jung stated that sharks were man's first enemy, before man had evolved into land-living creatures, and thereby is still a terrifying image in the archetypal imagery of the subconscious. That theory seemed valid to the woman, but it didn't help with her dreams. Finally, someone asked her, 'What do sharks mean to *you*?' Without thinking, she replied, 'Eating machines.' She then realized the extent of her anxiety over her recent weight gain, which she had tried to ignore, but which was inwardly 'consuming' her. She learned to control her overeating, and her shark dreams disappeared.

Crystal Ball Scrying

∞∞∞∞∞

Crystal balls call forth an image of a Gypsy in a sideshow tent, wearing scarves and demanding that silver cross her palm. Or perhaps it puts one in mind of the Wicked Witch of the West finding out Dorothy's whereabouts in her crystal ball. Crystallomancy is actually an ancient practice, dating back as far as the early Christian era, with roots in Jewish mysticism and the Kabbala. The Australian aborigines, the Mayans, the Incas and the North American Indians, as well as the tribal people of Borneo and New Guinea, have all practiced gazing.

Crystal ball gazing does not require a crystal ball at all. The ball is simply one instrument used to 'scry,' a type of divination involving observation. Any smooth, reflective surface, such as a bowl of water, a mirror or a lake are used. Nostradamus, the French sixteenth-century physician and astrologer, combined astrology and the visions he scryed in a bowl of water to make his predictions. In Celtic tradition, a girl would see her future husband in a mirror on Samhain, or New Year's Eve, the holiday now celebrated by witches as Halloween. The Greeks often went to springs to hear their oracles, scryed in a mirror held just below the surface of

the water. In the Bible, Joseph divined the future in a cup as well as in his dreams. In Egypt and India, pools of dark ink serve as a canvas upon which images may emerge. In fact, the Rorschach test is a form of scrying.

Scrying differs from other forms of divination in that omens are internal rather than external. For example, tea leaves and palms are physical patterns that need only to be interpreted; the images that appear in a crystal ball must be summoned by the diviner. John Melville writes in his classic book *Crystal Gazing and Clairvoyance* that there are three levels of gazing. In the first, the mind reproduces images already present in the subconscious of the gazer. In the second, the diviner receives images transferred telepathically from other people's thoughts or conversations. In the third, the true clairvoyant receives genuine information. According to Melville, only a crystal ball will show proper visions.

Most crystal balls found today are made of glass, but balls are traditionally made of polished beryl or quartz. Those are difficult to find and quite

*Many scryers prefer genuine crystal balls, smooth and globular, (**previous page**), though some seekers find that a surface of water (**below**), a faceted crystal (**opposite page**), or even a puddle of ink best reveal the answers sought by the querant.*

expensive. A glass ball should be as free from imperfections (such as air bubbles) as possible. Scryers treat their balls carefully, to keep the surface free from scratches, which could interfere with the images contained therein. The same care is taken with the bowls and mirrors used for divination. The bottoms of bowls and the backs of mirrors are blackened to enhance the visions.

THE RITES OF THE SCRYER

When using a crystal ball, the diviner first passes his or her right hand over it several times to clear and revitalize the energies. Then the left hand is passed over to enhance the crystal's receptiveness. This ritual aids in clearing the mind of the diviner, for increased sensitivity to the images. Should an oracle concerning a particular person be required, the diviner may invite that person into the room, sometimes even asking that the individual hold the ball briefly. Or the diviner may simply concentrate on an image of the person.

As the diviner gazes at the crystal ball, it will become cloudy or dull, signalling the coming of visions. The crystal may become extremely dark, suddenly brightening with a sharp image. Often, however, the ball offers only clouds, the color of which indicates different meanings. White clouds imply a 'yes' to any question that may have been asked, and a generally favorable disposition toward any situation. Black clouds mean no, unless they then give way to brightness, which points to a change for the better. Violet, green or blue clouds prognosticate joy, while red, orange or yellow warn of danger, illness, grief or some unpleasant surprise.

Ascending clouds indicate 'yes,' and descending mean 'no.' According to Melville, clouds moving to the right signify a spirit who has concern for the gazer. Clouds or shadows moving to the left indicate that the gazer should leave the ball for awhile. If an image appears to move toward the scryer, the foretold events or situation will come about rapidly. An image which moves away means that the situation, object or person symbolized by the image will soon be removed from the gazer's life. Images appearing on the left are actual physical occurrences, while images on the right are symbolic. If the scryer wishes to know about something far away in either time or space, he or she leans back and gazes aslant at the ball.

The symbols which appear to the scryer may be interpreted in the same manner as the images in a dream. Scryers are careful to distinguish between images originating on the first and second levels of divination and those which are a result of clairvoyance. Many believe, also, that demons and other unfriendly spirits use the balls to transmit misleading information, so a certain amount of caution is exercised.

The Gift of the Clairvoyant

⭕⭕⭕⭕⭕

Since the dawn of recorded time, some people have possessed a special power, a sixth sense that allows them to *see* or *know* things in ways that other people cannot. In ancient Greece, oracles foretold the death of kings. During the Middle Ages, Joan of Arc, a peasant girl, heard voices telling her to lead the fight against the English invaders. Abraham Lincoln dreamed of his own assassination. Legions of other people have experienced events that were less spectacular but nonetheless beyond the pale of everyday existence.

Today scientists study these unusual events under the heading of parapsychology. The miracles and strange visions of old are now considered extrasensory perception.

Four types of extrasensory perception, or ESP, are commonly studied:

Telepathy, or mind reading, is the transference of thought between people without the use of words. Some parapsychologists believe that telepathy occurs most often between people with a close emotional bond, such as identical twins or mother and child.

Yours Truly,
J. R. Francis

Clairvoyance, or second sight, is the knowledge of distant events or objects through means other than the five senses. Clairvoyance can take the form of a prolonged vision, but it most often is a brief mental glimpse of the event or object.

Precognition is the ability to perceive the future. This knowledge can occur in a dream or while awake.

Psychokinesis is the ability to use the mind's powers to change external matter.

The word psi is an umbrella term used to describe any type of psychic ability. The term comes from the 23rd letter of the Greek alphabet and represents an unknown quantity.

SEPARATING THE FRAUDS FROM THE SEERS

In 1882, Henry Sedgwick, a prominent philosopher, formed the Society for Psychical Research (SPR) in London to study psychic phenomena and to rationalize them in both religious and scientific terms. The other founding members included physicists and philosophers.

The following year Sedgwick met with William James, the eminent Harvard psychologist and philosopher, who in turn founded the American Society for Psychical Research in 1885. James, along with several other psychologists, focused on studying the claims of various mediums.

Rather than trying to prove the truth of spiritualists and mediums, the ASPR and the SPR sought to understand the paranormal in logical, rational terms. The members' standing in the scientific community accorded psychic phenomena a newfound respectability. However, the ASPR and SPR were fraught with difficulties almost immediately. Though they were experts in their own fields, no one knew how to conduct research on the paranormal. A major problem was separating frauds from the genuine article.

TESTING THE POWERS

Research of psychic phenomena began in earnest in the late 1920s, with the work of Professor Joseph Banks Rhine at Duke University. A professor in the psychology department, Rhine believed that the potential for psychic abilities existed in the general public and thus concentrated his energies on 'everyday people' rather than on the avowed psychic. As subjects for his

experiments, Rhine recruited students and faculty at Duke. He began his research with an experiment involving a shuffled deck of cards. Subjects were asked to guess the order of the cards. If they scored better than could be expected by chance, some unknown factor was believed to be responsible. Like other researchers of the day, Rhine used an ordinary deck of playing cards. However, he was worried that 52 cards was too large a number with which to work, reasoning that subjects might tend to pick favorite numbers or avoid numbers they associated with bad luck.

Rhine asked a colleague, Karl Zener, to design a new set of cards. The Zener cards, as Rhine promptly dubbed them, featured a total of 25 cards—five cards each of five different, yet simple, designs: a circle, a square, a star, a plus sign and a wavy line.

To test for telepathic powers, the sender (the person conducting the experiment) would concentrate on the card that he had turned up, while the subject recorded his impression of the card. Often the sender and subject were seated at the same table, but in some cases they were seated farther apart, sometimes even in different buildings. To test for clairvoyance, the subject tried to perceive the cards as they were being turned over, or he tried to predict the order of the cards in the shuffled deck. To test for precognition, the subject

Page 97: *Those people with the gifts of clairvoyance and precognition have rare insight on the mysterious workings of the hand of fate.*

Opposite page: The Progressive Thinker, *published by Mr JR Francis, circa 1900, was a publication that no spiritualist could do without.*

Above: *Scientists are unable to state conclusively why some people are able to transmit and receive thoughts without saying a word.*

attempted to predict what the order of the cards would be after they were shuffled.

According to the laws of probability and averages, a person would guess the correct answer, or hit, five times. In just one run through the deck, he might hit only one or twice, but over several trials the average would be about five hits. An average of nine hits, however, would be considered more than just chance.

After two years of study, Rhine found eight subjects who regularly scored above chance. The most successful of Rhine's subjects was a shy divinity student named Hubert Pearce. When Pearce exhibited an incredible ability at predicting the cards, Rhine devised a further series of tests that are still regarded as milestones in paranormal research. The results were remarkable, especially considering that Pearce and his experimenter, J Gaither Pratt, were in separate buildings.

With Pearce situated in a cubicle at the Duke library, Pratt would take a card from the deck and place it down without looking at it. Pearce, meanwhile, would record his impression of each card. Since Pratt did not look at the cards, this was a test of Pearce's clairvoyant ability. The results were astounding. Over a period of eight months, 1850 trials were conducted, and in one series of 12 runs of the Zener cards, Pearce scored as high as 13 hits per deck.

Although Rhine and his associates could offer no explanations for the results, they began to understand the psychology behind the psychic process. They discovered, for example, that mood affected psychic ability. In general, subjects scored higher when they were motivated. Rhine once offered Pearce $100 for every hit—and Pearce hit every card in the deck. On the other hand, subjects' scores declined when they were depressed or fatigued. Pearce did poorly after his fiancée broke off their engagement.

In 1934, Rhine published the results of his research in a monograph entitled *Extra-Sensory Perception*. Rhine was the first to coin the term, and he

Opposite page: *Carl Jung, noted Swiss psychologist and a student of Sigmund Freud.*

Below: *Parapsychologists are devoted to unraveling the mysterious powers of the human mind.*

Below, at bottom: *The Zener cards were designed in the 1920s and are still used today to test for telepathic abilities.*

selected it carefully, trying 'to make it sound as normal as may be.' As perception was a branch of psychology, Rhine hoped that ESP would be viewed as a serious science rather than as some strange, supernatural curiosity.

The general public was captivated by Rhine's treatise, and some members of the academic community were convinced of the validity of Rhine's work. *Extra-Sensory Perception*, however, was not without its detractors. Some psychologists criticized Rhine's statistical methodology, while others pointed out the possibility for a high margin of error.

Meanwhile, Gardner Murphy, a psychologist at Columbia University, was also studying psychic phenomena. Rhine referred his graduate students to Murphy, and in 1937 the two men founded *The Journal of Parapsychology*. The budding science soon attracted more students, and research centers were instituted at various universities. Rhine's book also came to the attention of the noted psychologist Carl Jung, who praised the work and encouraged Rhine to continue his research even though he would undoubtedly encounter criticism.

Jung had been fascinated by the paranormal since childhood, growing up in an environment that encouraged him to view psychic phenomena as a natural part of life. As an adult he studied astrology and the I *Ching*, and quite naturally followed Rhine's experiments with interest. Over the years Jung developed his theory of synchronicity to explain psychic events. According to Jung, synchronicity refers to a 'meaningful coincidence' of outer and inner events that are not themselves causally related. As an example of his theory, Jung referred to the pendulum clock in the palace of Frederick the Great at Sans Souci, which stopped when the emperor died.

As Jung had predicted to Rhine, the science of parapsychology would be the subject of criticism for the next 25 years. In spite of the critics, Rhine and his colleagues persevered until 1965, when Rhine retired and the laboratory at Duke was closed. Today parapsychology is studied at over 100 colleges and universities throughout the United States. One of the major centers of study is the University of Utrecht in the Netherlands.

Over the years the methods for testing psychic ability have become more technologically advanced. Hand-kept records have been replaced

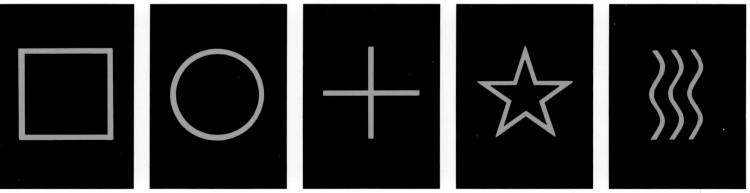

with computers, and Zener cards have been supplanted by Random Event Generators (REGs).

One of these first REGs was used by Dr Helmut Schmidt at Boeing Research Laboratory. The machine was driven by a piece of radioactive strontium 90. As the particle decayed, it emitted electrons that lit four colored lights at random. The subjects were asked to predict which light would be lit next. In one series of tests conducted with Schmidt's REG, subjects correctly predicted the light 26.7 percent of the time. The chance of correctly guessing would be about 25 percent, and while 26.7 percent seems only slightly higher, from a statistical point of view the difference is significant.

Free response experiments are another method of psi testing. One of the best-known free response experiments was conducted by Harold Puthoff, Bonnar Cox and Russell Targ of the Stanford Research Institute (later SRI International) in 1974. Puthoff and Cox drove around for a half an hour, while the subject, Pat Price, a retired police commissioner from Burbank, California, was locked in an electronically shielded room.

The test was designed to study a phenomenon known as remote viewing. After Puthoff and Cox had driven for half an hour, Price was to describe

Above: Studies show that fewer passengers ride a train when it is about to wreck. Researcher WE Cox hypothesized that some people have premonitions, or simply bad feelings, and decide to stay home on those days.

their location to Russell Targ, who was in the room with him to monitor the experiment. Price was able to describe the scene *before* Cox and Puthoff arrived—and they had no destination in mind as they were driving—with amazing accuracy: 'What I am looking at is a little boat jetty or a little boat dock along the bay. I see some motor launches, some little sailing ships.' Price also noted 'a definite feeling of Oriental architecture that seems to be fairly adjacent to where they are.'

Twenty minutes later Cox and Puthoff arrived at the Redwood City Marina, a harbor and boat dock about five miles away from SRI. Nearby was an Oriental restaurant.

Targ and Puthoff continued their experiments for the next several years, increasing the distance between subject and location. Their results were mixed, but one woman, Hella Hammid, described five out of nine sites correctly, prompting Targ and Puthoff to put her to a difficult test. From a submarine two miles off the California coast, Hammid was asked to identify a site somewhere in the San Francisco Bay area—a large oak tree on a cliff overlooking Stanford University. She correctly identified the tree and the cliff, and she reported that the experimenter, who was climbing the tree, was behaving in an 'unscientific manner.'

COMMON PSYCHIC EXPERIENCE IN EXTRAORDINARY CIRCUMSTANCES

Though virtually impossible to verify, evidence of psi ability is, of course, found beyond the confines of the laboratory. Researchers have attempted to document the reports of psychic experiences that often accompany stories of disasters such as earthquakes, plane crashes and so on. After studying rail accidents, WE Cox noted that the trains involved in accidents typically carried fewer passengers on the day of the accident than they did on other days. Cox hypothesized that many people may have had a premonition—perhaps subconscious—about the impending wreck and therefore stayed home.

One disaster that has been extensively studied is the 1912 sinking of the *Titanic*. Ian Stevenson, a psychiatrist and parapsychologist at the University of Virginia, studied psychic phenomenon associated with the *Titanic* and discovered 19 instances of apparent psi ability. The subjects ranged from people who had loved ones aboard the ocean liner to those who had no connection to the passengers or crew, and the psi experiences included dreams and hallucinations. An 11-year-old girl, whose mother was onboard, experienced a 'strange sense of doom.' Two days before the *Titanic* sank, a woman started screaming hysterically, 'It's going to sink' as the great ocean liner passed by the waving crowds on the Isle of Wight.

Another catastrophe that was widely predicted was a coal-waste avalanche in the mining village of Aberfan, Wales. On the morning of 21 October 1966, a 600-foot mound of coal waste from the adjacent mountains shook and then roared down upon the village. Trees were uprooted, houses were swept away and the school was buried under the black mass—just as 10-year-old schoolgirl Eryl Mai Jones had seen in a dream the day before. 'I dreamed I went to school,' she told her mother, 'and there was no school there. Something black had come down all over it.'

Reports of visions of the tragedy at Aberfan were reported all over England. Prior to the disaster, an amateur artist in southwestern England couldn't shake the feeling that a disaster involving coal dust was about to happen. Several other people had nightmares that they were suffocating in blackness, others dreamed of children running to escape an avalanche of black, and one man saw the word 'Aberfan' spelled out in a dream.

London psychiatrist JC Barker instigated a search for anyone who had experienced a premonition of the coal avalanche. Dr Barker investigated 76 people claiming to have foreseen the disaster. He immediately rejected 16 as inconclusive, but of the remaining 60 he discovered that more than

Right: *Vinolia Toilet Soap couldn't keep the Titanic afloat when it struck an iceberg in 1912. Nineteen incidents of apparent psi ability were reported in connection with the oceanliner's disaster.*

Below: *Adelaide Worthington, an actress living in New York City, was one of many people who had a premonition of the Titanic disaster. Miss Worthington's fiancé lost his life in that tragic mishap.*

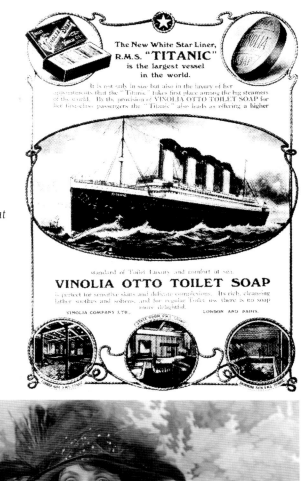

half had experienced the sensation of impending disaster in a dream. In roughly a third of the cases, the people had documented the experience in a letter or diary before the coal slide occurred.

Convinced of the existence of psychic abilities, Dr Barker saw the need for a clearinghouse for predictions, and in 1967 established the British Premonitions Bureau to analyze and research predictions from known psychics as well as from the general public. Soon after, a similar agency, the Central Premonitions Registry, was formed in the United States.

TRANSFORMATION OF CONSCIOUSNESS

Because dreams were the channel in which so many people received information about the unknown, researchers began to explore a new area of study called Altered States Research (ASR). ASR examines the theory that when an individual is in a

Opposite page: Volcanologists working at the Hawaiian Volcano Observatory on the island of Hawaii were surprised to receive several calls from persons abroad warning of a major eruption of Kilauea in June 1986.

Below: ASR experiments test the hypothesis that while in altered states of consciousness, such as sleep, hypnosis and meditation, individuals are more sensitive to communication from deep within the mind.

modified state of awareness—be it sleep or a trance—he or she is more sensitive to communication from deep within the mind.

In addition to examining psi abilities during sleep, researchers have studied induced altered states of consciousness, such as hypnosis, drugs, meditation and biofeedback. One of the most successful experiments involving hypnotism was conducted in the early 1960s by Milan Rylz, a Czechoslovakian biochemist. Rylz hypnotized Pavel Stepanek into believing that he had psychic powers. For more than a decade, Stepanek exhibited incredible psi ability. He was an especially high scorer at card guessing, sometimes at odds of 500,000 to one.

In the 1970s, a new area of research was developed called ganfeld, a German term that means 'total field.' Parapsychologist Charles Honorton was the first to conceive of the ganfeld environment, which duplicates a highly relaxed dream state. Isolated from the external environment, the subject lies in a darkened room, his eyes covered with halved table tennis balls and his ears filled with synthesized white noise. In this alert but relaxed state, he is deprived of outside stimulation and focuses on the images that come from within.

THE USE OF PSYCHIC POWER TO SOLVE CRIMES

Some of the most sensational examples of psychic abilities are found in the headlines of grocery store tabloids proclaiming that a psychic has solved a crime that has baffled police for months. While these stories are frequently more fiction than fact, there have been numerous documented examples of people using psychic abilities to solve a crime.

Two of the best known psychics are from the Netherlands—Gerard Croiset and Peter Hurkos. Born in 1909, Croiset had an uneasy existence. He found it difficult to hold down a job, and he was twice arrested by the Gestapo. Life finally turned around for him in 1945, when he met Willem Tenhaeff, an unpaid lecturer in parapsychology at the University of Utrecht.

As is often the case with psychics, Croiset's success rate for solving crimes was relatively small. Even so, some cases were remarkable for their accuracy, at least in certain details. Croiset is perhaps best known for the case involving four-year-old Edith Kiecorius of Brooklyn, New York, who had disappeared on 22 February 1961.

Croiset agreed to assist in the search for the missing girl, and before he had left Holland for New York, he had an image of the situation. The girl was dead. Her body would be found in a tall building with a billboard on top near an elevated railroad and a river. The murderer was a small, sharp-

Above: As predicted by Dutch psychic Gerard Croiset, Amsterdam police found the body of missing six-year-old Wimpje Slee in one of the city's canals.

faced man, about 54 or 55, from southern Europe. He was wearing grey. Upon arriving in New York, he had a clearer vision, declaring that the building had five floors and the body would be found on the second floor.

As Croiset had predicted, the body was found on the second floor of a building near the Hudson River and an elevated railroad. The police arrested and later convicted a small, sharp-nosed, swarthy man dressed in grey checks. Croiset did miss on a few accounts. The building was four stories, not five, and the suspect was from England, not southern Europe.

Police solved the case without the assistance of Croiset—they discovered the body in a search unrelated to the clues Croiset had provided.

Peter Hurkos was far more flamboyant and theatrical than his countryman Croiset. Hurkos' psychic abilities emerged in 1941 after he had fallen four stories from a building he had been painting. The 30-year-old worker was taken to the hospital unconscious. When he awoke four days later he had amnesia and was suffering from a concussion and possible neurological damage. Shortly after regaining consciousness, he had a vision of his son, Benny, in a burning room. Five days later Benny was rescued from a fire.

After the accident, Hurkos' ability to concentrate was impaired to the point that he could not work or even read a book, but he suddenly seemed to have psychic abilities. He wasted no time in putting his new talents to use, giving shows for the public.

In 1947, he was asked to help solve the murder of a Dutch coal miner. Hurkos felt the dead man's coat, declaring that the man had been killed by his

DOOR USED AS EXIT BY WOMAN

POOL

SHOOTING OCCURRED AT HEAD OF STAIRWAY

DOOR BY WHICH POLICE GAINED ENTRANCE

ELLI S, ST. BARBE R SHOP

stepfather and the gun would be found on the roof of the dead man's house. Police did indeed find the gun where Hurkos had foreseen. Fingerprints on the gun led to the stepfather's conviction. Within a year Hurkos was famous throughout Europe and soon emigrated to the United States, where he became equally well known as a psychic advisor to Hollywood celebrities.

Though he didn't usually work on criminal cases, in 1964 Hurkos agreed to investigate the Boston Strangler case. For six days he studied two large boxes of items related to the case, and pronounced that the Strangler would be found at Boston College. The police showed him a letter to the Boston College School of Nursing from a man who wanted to interview—and perhaps marry—a typical nurse.

Upon seeing the letter, Hurkos declared that the letter writer was the killer. He described the man as a 52-year-old woman-hater who spoke with a French accent. He had a pointed nose, thin, receding hair and a prominent Adam's apple. Hurkos' dreams revealed even more details about the man: he slept on a cot, showered with his shoes on, and kept a diary that would reveal that he was the Boston Strangler.

Above: San Francisco police, with the assistance of psychic Henry Mikeskell, were able to solve the case of a mysterious murder that occurred in that city in June 1930. The psychic's clues led the police to arrest a woman who, as sensed by Mikeskell, had fled the scene of the crime.

Acting on Hurkos' clues, the police discovered a man they called Thomas P O'Brien. (His real name was withheld from the public.) In appearance and habits, O'Brien matched the description given by Hurkos, but the police had no evidence with which they could arrest him. They were, however, able to have O'Brien temporarily committed to a mental hospital for observation. In turn, O'Brien had himself voluntarily committed, making it impossible for him to be tried for murder.

Several months later, Albert DeSalvo was arrested for rape, diagnosed as schizophrenic and committed to the same institution as O'Brien. DeSalvo began to boast that he was the Boston Strangler, and he spoke with enough knowledge of the crimes that police were convinced that he truly was the killer. However, since he had been declared legally insane, DeSalvo, like O'Brien, could not be tried for murder, and the case of the Boston Strangler was closed without a trial.

The fact that Hurkos apparently had identified the wrong man tended to obscure his psychic accomplishments in the case. From simply examining evidence he had an amazing knowledge of the crimes, and his dreams of O'Brien and his surroundings were incredibly accurate.

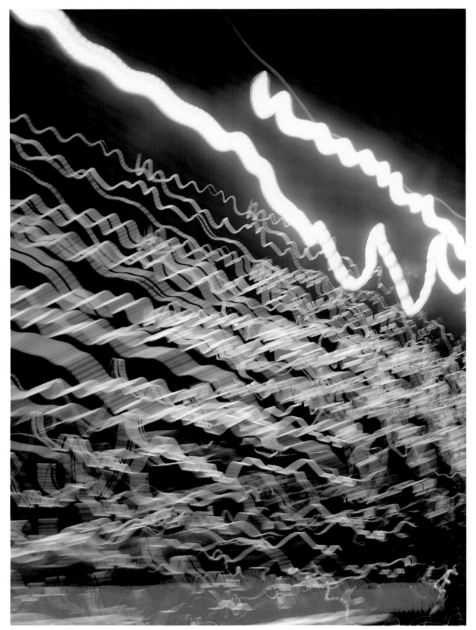

Several years later Hurkos was again called upon to assist with a heinous crime—the 1969 murder of actress Sharon Tate by Charles Manson. Hurkos claimed to have played an important part in solving the case, but police investigators minimized his significance.

The stories of Hurkos and Croiset typify the problems with using psychics to solve crimes. The details seldom lead to solving the crime and often are way off base. Dorothy Allison, a New Jersey psychic, has worked on over 4000 cases but claims to have solved less than 100. What cannot be ignored, however, is that in some instances, the psychics' predictions are correct, albeit grim, portraits of reality.

Allison first attracted public attention in December 1967, when she announced that she knew the whereabouts of five-year-old Michael Kurcsics. The boy was dead, she said, and his body would be found in a drainpipe. His shoes were on the wrong feet and he was wearing a green snowsuit. In the distance she saw a gray building, gold letters and the number eight.

Two months later, the boy's body was found in a drainpipe in Clifton, New Jersey. As Allison had predicted, he was wearing a green snowsuit and, under his boots, his sneakers were on the wrong feet. Nearby were a grey building, a factory with gold lettering and PS 8 elementary school.

In 1975, Dorothy Allison, among other psychics, assisted in the Patty Hearst kidnapping case. Her results were mixed. Although she could never exactly pinpoint the missing heiress' location, Allison was able to provide general information about Hearst's whereabouts and activities.

The following year Allison once again solved a missing person case. Like the case of Michael Kurcsics nine years earlier, this case began with a missing person and ended in murder. As before, Allison's clues led to the discovery of the body of 18-year-old Deborah Sue Kline. In this instance, she predicted that the body would be found on a hill. She also saw the color yellow, a dump, a shoe and a plastic swimming pool. Allison made the startling prediction that the case would soon be solved. Two men had been involved in the crime; one would confess and implicate the other.

Allison's vision was correct. A man named Richard Lee Dodson confessed and led the police to Fannettsburg Mountain. All of Allison's clues were present: yellow signs marked the route, a dump was nearby, the shoe belonged to the victim—and she was buried under a plastic swimming pool.

ESP THEORIES

The first challenge confronting the parapsychologists is to prove that psychic phenomena do indeed exist, and even as they work to document the existence of paranormal events, researchers must also attempt to explain *how* these events occur, for they contradict the laws of physics. Some researchers, however, contend that scientific theory can be used to explain the paranormal and have pointed to physical descriptions of the universe as models for paranormal activity.

One of the earliest models for ESP was found in the laws of electromagnetism, which describe how some signals for light, x-rays and so on travel in waves from a source to a receiver. At one end of the electromagnetic spectrum are short, high-frequency waves and at the other end are long, low-frequency waves, such as radio signals from a distant galaxy. Some parapsychologists hypothesized that psi waves were part of the spectrum, and like most electromagnetic waves cannot be sensed by human beings, except for those who can tune in their psychic receivers.

This model has been rejected by most parapsychologists today because psi waves were never found and the model failed to explain the faster-than-light speeds and undiminished power associated with precognition and telepathy.

A more recent model is based on multidimensional geometry. In this model, the paranormal exists outside, but interacts with, the four dimensions of time and space (height, width, depth). Some mathematicians have postulated that there are more than the four known dimensions, possibly as many as 26, and that the psi world belongs to one of these dimensions. The problem with this theory is that there is no *physical* evidence to support it.

A current model for psychic phenomena has its roots in quantum mechanics. According to the laws of quantum mechanics, units of matter at the subatomic level behave in a seemingly paradoxical manner, acting as neither particle nor wave. In fact, matter cannot even be said to exist; rather, matter is expressed in terms of mathematical probability and is said to have a 'tendency to exist.'

The paradoxical nature of quantum mechanics is demonstrated in the following famous example: When two particles—an electron and its antimatter equivalent, a positron—collide, the two particles are annihilated and two photons are created, each one speeding off in a different direction. Quantum mechanics states that photon A does not possess properties such as spin or velocity

Opposite page and below: No one understands what form psychic energy takes—whether it is wave or particle energy or something that is still entirely unknown to science.

until it is noted by an observer. The moment that photon A is observed and takes on a spin, photon B acquires the opposite spin. In simple terms, photon B seems to know what photon A is doing, suggesting that the universe is connected in some hidden way.

The same concept is applied to psychic behavior, the implication being that human consciousness exists at the subatomic level, which explains why a psychic can know instantly of an event across the world.

As the study of parapsychology enters the 1990s, support from the academic world is mixed. Although some scientists see little value in continued research, the American Association of Science recently admitted the Parapsychological Association as an affiliated member society, and the National Institute of Mental Health, an American governmental body, has given grant support for the medical research of telepathic dreams. In Great Britain, intensive study of parapsychology is under way at Cambridge and a poll in *New Scientist* revealed keen interest in the subject. Worldwide, on the popular front, parapsychology continues to fascinate and amaze.

The Mystic Oracle of Domino Divination

Dominoes originated in the Middle East, but are found all over the world, in many different cultures. Like some other forms of divination, such as dice and tarot cards, they are also deployed as playing pieces in games. Because of their ancient beginnings, it is uncertain whether these objects were first used for games or for prophecy. If first they were sacred divinatory tools, the first person to use them in play was obviously an unbeliever.

When used as divinatory tools, the dominoes are placed face down, and mixed about thoroughly before one is chosen. Some diviners insist on chosing the most distant domino, but others trust Fate to provide the guiding hand. After the reading, the domino is replaced face down and the dominoes are shuffled before another may be drawn.

Consulting the dominoes more than once a month, or on Mondays or Fridays, may result in doubtful divination, or worse, an adverse fulfillment of a prophecy. Three dominoes are the prescribed limit for an individual at one sitting,

unless a duplicate domino is drawn. The duplicate underscores the prophecy of the domino.

DECODING THE AUGURIES

Double blank This domino is considered the worst of all, bringing total disappointment to all persons except those who thrive on dishonesty and deceit. Whoever has gained anything by fraud is likely to retain it by turning up this domino. Other people will find it bad in business and in love. It may mean loss of valuables, or even a job.

Double ace This is a symbol of happiness both in love and music. It not only promises harmony and affection, but also portends financial gains and security.

Two-blank For a man, dishonesty and ill luck are designated by this domino. If a woman turns it up, the meaning is applicable to her boyfriend or husband. A son might be dissipating his talents. If travel is the objective of the consultant, the predic-

Previous page: The domino is an ancient article, used both as a toy and as a divinatory tool.

Below: Lucky is the querant who draws the five-three domino, for it portends a life relatively free of strife.

tions are excellent, indicating a very pleasant and safe journey.

Two-one For a woman, two-one denotes an early marriage that would bring her wealth. However, she might become a widow and remarry, this time for many happy years. For a young man, there are no promises of wedding bells, just the life of a carefree and popular bachelor. In business, guard against an unbalanced budget.

Double two Success in business and a happy home life. For those who marry, children will add to their happiness. Thrift leads them to prosperity.

Three-blank An indication of quarrels. For a man, marriage would be tempestuous. At social gatherings, there will be debates of controversial subjects.

Three-one Warning that scandal may cause unhappiness, if one is influenced too much by what others think.

Three-two A lucky combination for love, marriage and money (especially investments and speculation), A propitious time for travel. Special care should be given to children at this time lest they feel neglected.

Double three Large sums of money and good

fortune in abundance will present themselves.

Four-blank Disappointments in love for both men and women. Neither will want to marry, despite the messiness of broken engagements. Anyone who has a secret should not divulge it. If the consultant is pregnant, this domino presages twins.

Four-one Promise of married bliss with an ample sufficiency of money. Finances will increase with the advent of each additional child. Excellent sign of prosperity.

Four-two A period of change is denoted by this domino. It may refer to family, money, occupation, almost anything. The change may be slight or it may be greatly different from the present status. Those in love may have a change of heart. Business that is slow will begin to improve. Whatever the circumstances may be, the four-two indicates a change.

Double four For artisans this is a lucky, fortunate prognostication. For all other people it is unfortunate as far as work or progress is concerned, but a wonderful time to socialize, relax and have fun. A wedding is predicted.

Five-blank Insincerity, imprudence and self-seeking abounds. One must be very cautious. Budgets must be carefully guarded, especially against an urge to gamble.

Five-one Money may be a disappointment, but family and friends are not.

Five-two Marriage is not a good idea at this time. For newly-weds, marital misunderstandings may occur that will take a long time to mend. Patience and tolerance will bring eventual happiness if the consultant is a woman. For a man, he would do well to marry a woman who is industrious and thrifty. If he intends to change his business connections, or venture into something new, it is best to take time, not be hasty, and investigate every channel thoroughly.

Five-three This domino portends a smooth, comfortable way of life, calm and well-adjusted. Material goods will not be excessive, but all needs will be met.

Five-four A young woman will not compromise her ideals in love or business. Her every word and action are made with conviction. She must always check her associates to insure that she is not being hoodwinked. This domino also threatens loss of money, a poor time for investments.

Double five Great success in any field is predicted. Enterprise will bring in lots of money.

Six-blank An unhappy sign that signifies financial strain and news of death, possibly of a family member or someone else of importance.

Six-one To the young who draw this domino, two marriages are awaiting you in the future. To those already married, good fortune will attend them in their later years. Children of these families do not always stay close to their families since their interests take them far away. One child may prefer the proximity of parental love.

Six-two A lucky domino for people who are scrupulous and fair in their dealings. It threatens trou-

Above: Domino divination is the preferred method used by the oft-consulted San Francisco psychic Melinda Quinn.

ble for the dishonest and the unfair. To a married couple, it foretells prosperity and unity of family.

Six-three The most fortunate draw for lovers. Their marriage vows are the beginning of a fruitful family life and many prosperous years. Often this draw is considered the best one for riches.

Six-four This domino augurs a deep understanding of the rhythms of nature, the cycles of prosperity and leanness, and the intricacies of human nature.

Six-five Perseverance is the key. If disappointment is about money matters, one may have to start over again. If poor health is the trouble, patiently strive for healing. If disappointed in love, there is someone else much more worthy of affection and devotion. If a business is expanding, every detail should be double-checked.

Double six This domino promises riches and honor to a woman on the threshold of a new experience. This is the only sign that is favorable toward wealth accrued through speculative ventures.

The Power of the Tarot

CRORORO

The reading of tarot cards is an ancient practice of unknown origins. It is almost certain that their purpose was one of foretelling the future, and tarot reading today continues to be a popular form of divination.

Noted Swiss psychologist Carl Gustav Jung was interested in all aspects of parapsychology. He was especially intrigued by the repeated occurrence of certain symbols that appeared in the dreams of people cross-culturally. He believed that there exists a collective subconscious, a reservoir of universal symbols, from which the subconscious mind is able to draw. He called these universal symbols 'archetypes.' The collective subconscious would explain certain psychic phenomena.

Some authorities claim that the tarot cards were adapted from the legendary 'Book of Thoth' used by ancient Egyptians. By the fourteenth century, the decks had surfaced in Europe, where they were called *tarots* and consisted of 78 cards. Of these, 56 were suit cards similar to those of modern decks, except that the suits were swords, rods, cups and coins instead of spades, diamonds, hearts and clubs, respectively. Each suit had four court cards, king, queen, knight, and knave (jack),

as well as the number cards from 10 to ace in descending order. These suit cards are known as the 'lesser arcana' (from 'arcane'—secret). The 'greater arcana' is comprised of the additional 22 trump cards on which are pictured powerful, archetypal images. A list of the most commonly used images follows: the Juggler, the High Priestess, the Empress, the Emperor, the Hierophant, the Lovers, the Chariot, Justice, the Hermit, Fortune, Strength, the Hanged Man, Death, Temperance, the Devil, Lightning, the Stars, the Moon, the Sun, Judgment, the World and the Fool.

The original designs were 'one way,' which meant they could be inverted when they were dealt. The inverted cards would lend an ominous tone to the reading. The full deck of 78 cards was used chiefly for predicting the outcome of future events or for reconstructing the past.

As card games which used the lesser arcana grew in popularity, the decks were reduced to 56 cards. Eventually the knight was dropped from the court cards, and their designs were made 'double ended.' The suits were changed by the French to hearts, clubs, diamonds and spades. The 'spots' on the number cards were left 'one way' but the numbers were reproduced in both directions to facilitate group play. Of the remaining 52 cards that make up today's decks, the fool, or joker, is the only remnant of the greater arcana in modern playing cards.

There are many systems, both widely known and obscure, for reading the cards. We will look at two of the more direct which have stood the test of time. The first uses the modern 52-card deck. The second uses the full 78 cards of the tarot. In both cases, certain guidelines must be followed in order to secure an accurate reading.

Each card bears a traditional meaning and various modified interpretations with which the reader should be familiar. Not only are there meanings associated with each card as it stands alone, but for each card as it relates to the layout as well. Knowing the impact of one card on another clarifies the suggestion of the first card.

It is not necessary for the reader to know the question of the querant, but the querant should reflect on the question while shuffling and drawing the cards. The chosen cards are then laid out, in order, in the form of a cross, a square or a circle. The willingness of the participant to gain insight from the tarot will surely enhance the reading, as will a skilled reader. A knowledgeable reader studies a wide range of medieval symbolism.

The most common symbols are of medieval origin, such as the castle, chalice, tower, king, queen and knave. The suits—rods, cups, swords and coins—represent different segments of medieval society: the peasantry, the clergy, the nobility and merchants, respectively. These images are powerful archetypes that speak to and shock the subconscious mind, and clear whatever psychic or emotional blocks exist.

Many modern occultists have modified the images on the cards to reflect contemporary con-

Previous page: Beautiful and colorful, the ancient tarot cards will yield their secrets to the learned and earnest reader.

These pages: Practitioners of the tarot employ several different formations when laying out their 'spreads.' The circular spread (below) provides a general forecast for the next 12 months. The first card forecasts the first month, the second card, the second month and so on, with the 13th card giving a general impression of the entire year.

The Celtic cross (opposite page) is probably the most useful and versatile of all the tarot spreads and may be used to answer specific or general questions. The entire deck can be used, or the greater arcana can be used alone.

cerns, personalizing the decks for women or men, and even omitting some cards or changing the nature of the decks.

THE LESSER ARCANA

Following is a general interpretation of each of the lesser arcana. The **aces** signify correspondence or news. **Twos** herald misunderstandings, quarrels or arguments. **Threes** imply improvement, progress, success, quietude and tranquility. **Fours** announce travel, outings, celebrations or sleepless nights due to overindulgence in alcohol. **Fives** are the cards of order, exactitude, resolutions and decisions. **Sixes** reflect a state of prosperity, abundance, general well-being and ease at home or in the country. **Sevens** and **eights** refer to male or female children.

Nines and **tens** must be looked at by suit. The nine of swords signifies disaster, sickness with a strong possibility of death, troubles and mourning. The nine of rods predicts a delay. Nine of cups is a favorable card, bringing pleasant and propitious things. The nine of coins brings festivities or outings. The ten of swords brings great suffering. The ten of rods implies the country, while the ten of cups, the city. The ten of coins connotes money.

The **Knaves** or **Jacks** represent young people, soldiers, lovers, seducers or rivals. The **Knights** indicate that gambling winnings will be greater

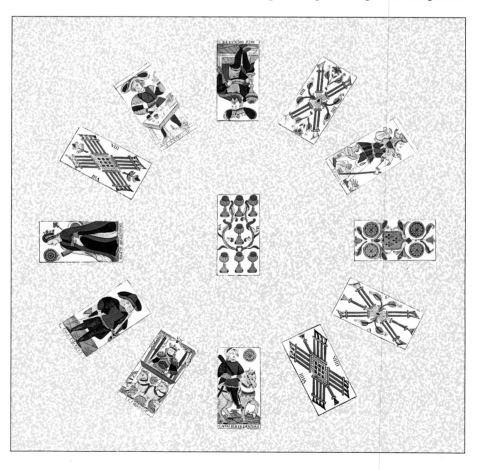

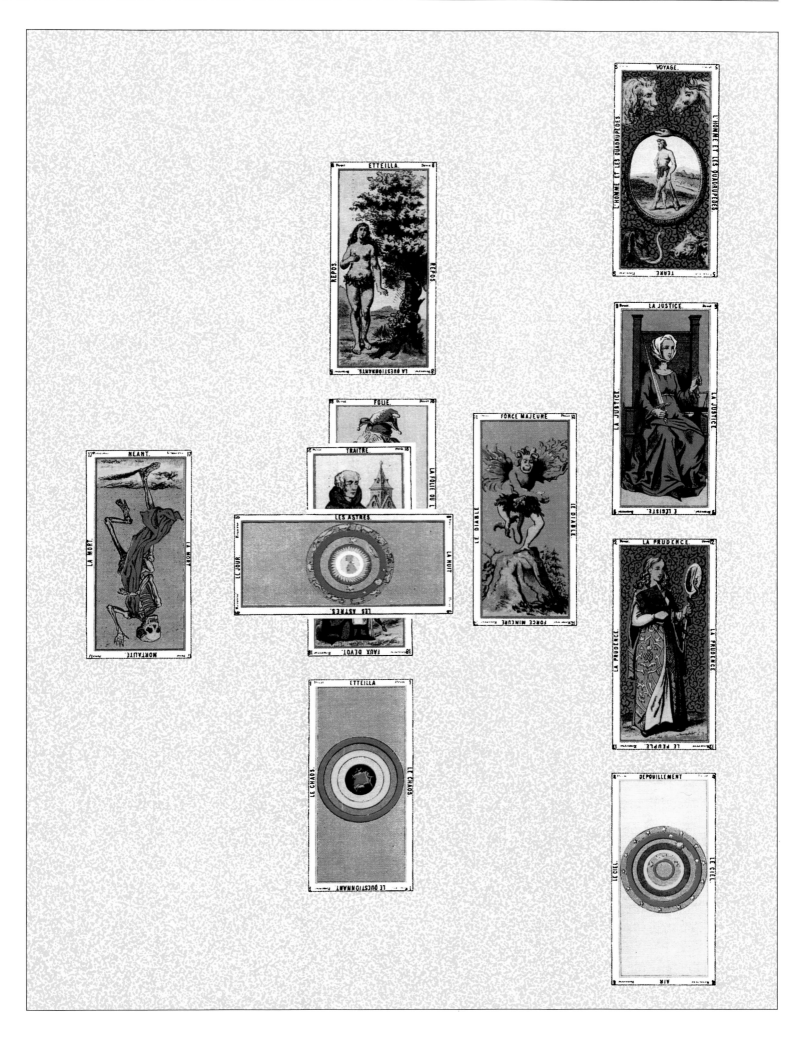

than losses. The **Queens** represent intriguing women of shifting moods and unpredictable actions. The **Kings** symbolize the law, officials, persons in authority, parents or the elderly.

In addition to these isolated meanings, the reading can be enhanced by the cards' relative position to others. Some authorities recommend that the reader have a thorough understanding of the seeker's question; others disagree, believing that the cards themselves know.

The lesser arcana represent the stages in a person's life. The first 11 cards tend to look outward, as an innocent (the Fool) moves toward middle life. The Wheel of Fortune marks the midway point. The second 11 cards are more introspective and contemplative as the individual approaches the end of his life and the symbol of the World.

Below: *The seven-pointed star is used to predict events for the next seven days. The cards on the outside of the star are dealt face down, while the significator is placed face up in the center. The other cards are then turned up and interpreted.*

THE GREATER ARCANA

The greater arcana typically are used to tell fortunes. One of the easiest and most direct spreads for tarot reading is the horseshoe spread. First the deck should be put in order, with every card right side up. Then with both the reader and the querant concentrating on the cards, the reader should shuffle the cards, and random cards turned so that inverted cards may be cast. The querant should then shuffle the deck a final time and return the cards to the reader. At this point, the deck is ready to be dealt in any formation. *At right* is an example of the horseshoe spread.

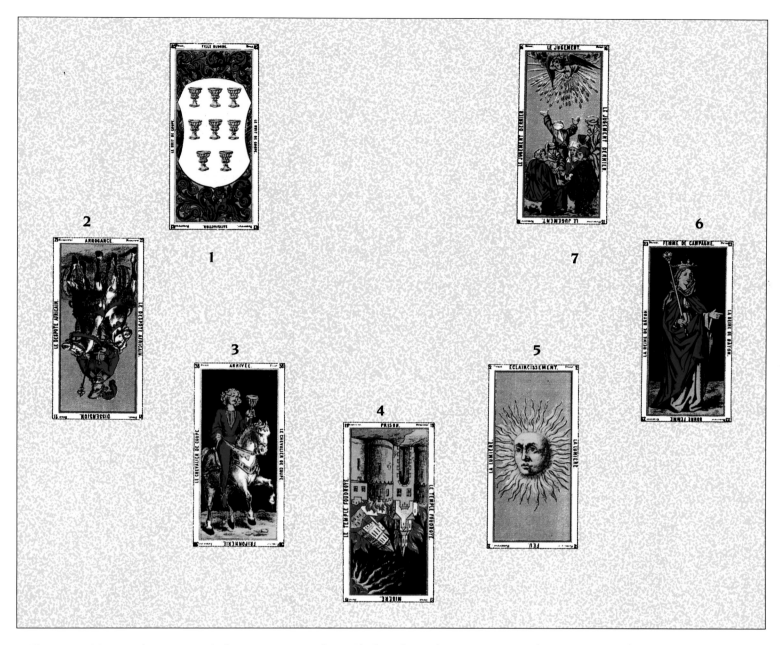

These positions refer to past influences (1), present circumstances (2), general future prospects (3), best course of action (4), the attitudes of others (5), possible obstacles (6), and final outcome (7).

The seven-pointed star spread can be dealt on any day of the week and used to forecast the events of the next seven days. The circular spread gives a general prognostication of the next 12 months from the date of the reading. For the 21-card layout the cards are dealt in three lines of seven from right to left and top to bottom. The Celtic cross is perhaps the most useful spread for divination. It can be employed for specific or general questions or for giving an overview of the coming year. Either the whole deck or just the lesser arcana is suitable for this spread. Consulting the tarot in the Celtic cross layout gives a well-rounded response to the querant, because it takes into account the querant's present state of mind, external influences such as friends and family, the querant's own hopes and fears, and the final outcome based on the collective impression of the cards.

Above: *The horseshoe is the most straightforward of the tarot spreads. It is useful for answering specific questions and is typically used with the greater arcana alone. A significator is not required.*

Some layouts require that a significator be chosen. This card should represent the querant and correspond with the subject in complexion, sex and personality. The following traditional significators are appropriate: queen of cups for a fair-haired young woman; queen of coins for a fair, mature woman (especially if she is affluent); queen of rods for a dark woman with an air of danger about her; queen of swords for a dark and sad woman; knight of cups for a fair young man or any young man in love; knight of coins for a wealthy young man; knight of rods for a dark young man; knave of rods for a young man who seems dangerous in character; king of cups for a fair-haired, mature man; king of coins for an affluent, mature man; king of swords for a mature man in a position of power and influence; and king of rods is the significator for a dark or dangerous mature man.

Some tarot readers do not find it necessary for the significator to correspond *in appearance* with the querant as long as the significator card matches the querant's personality traits.

Conclusion

M ankind has performed these rituals and practiced these arts of augury for thousands of years now. Some people believe that every time an action is performed with belief and seriousness, that action gains power. Perhaps that is the case with the various methods of foretelling described in the previous pages, which have been performed millions of times and believed in by millions of people in every culture. They have become powerful methods by which to approach the unknown.

Now, after the Age of Reason, people at last seem more willing to believe the same things as the ancients, and to believe that there is room enough in this world for science, logic *and* the mysterious and unexplainable.

Understanding and explaining such baffling and perplexing mysteries is not easy work. Scientists and psychologists are turning their attention toward proving the existence of these phenomenon, but many people are skeptical. Those who have believed all along will nod and smile politely, because they never needed to have anything proven to them. They have experienced, or perhaps only witnessed, the unexplainable, and that